UNDERSTANDING DIVERSITY

In learning, communication, and personal development

Berit Bergström

The author has previously published:

EVERY CHILD HAS SPECIFIC NEEDS, 2001, Runa Publisher
PEDAGOGIC TANGO (co Siv Saarukka), 2004, Runa Publisher

Originally published in Swedish by Recito Publisher Printed by
Bording Boras 2015
ISBN 978-91-7517-776-2
Bokutgivning.se forlag@bokutgivning.se www.bokutgivning.se
Recito Publishing Co. info@recito.se www.recito.se

First Edition Printing

Cover: Emelie Jonsson
Graphic design: Ulla Lindberg
Typesetting: Emilie Jonsson
English translation: Clarice M. Yentsch & Janet W. Campbell
Cover adapted from the original by Cori Convertito

ISBN-13: 978-91-639-4514-4

CONTENTS

FOREWORD

Three wise women have deeply influenced my life's braid -- the three strands being self, relationship, and work. These extraordinary women are Sandra Seagal, who channeled the theory of Human Dynamics and two amazing practitioners, Linda O'Toole in the USA and Berit Bergström in Sweden. The author Berit Bergström has guided the development of Human Dynamics Theory into models and teaching methods for education not only in Sweden, but in multiple places in the world.

For me it began with a 5-day introductory seminar on Human Dynamics in 1992 hosted by Kevin London, then the head of Human Resources at National Semiconductor in Portland, Maine. Kevin and I were co-chairs of the Community Integration Component for Maine's NSF-funded Statewide Systemic Initiative to radically improve Science, Technology, Engineering, and Mathematics (STEM) education. We helped develop the Maine Mathematics and Science Alliance which celebrates 25 years this year in 2017.

Kevin piqued my interest when he indicated that energy patterns were so fundamental they could be observed in newborn babies. As a research scientist, I was skeptical. By day 5 of the seminar I was a believer. I emerged knowing about myself and about my youngest son Carlton, then 20. The school system had failed him; I as a parent had also failed him because his learning process was different than my own. As Berit explains "When I got to know the different processes, I realized how blind and deaf I had been for the students who had learning processes and communication preferences other than my own ... misunderstanding can be devastating to the child."

Berit goes on "The most important thing for me was to consciously create a safe environment for all students to meet their various needs in the learning situation." I echo her sentiment.

The overarching goal is to create awareness in ourselves and others. The balanced interplay of the three principles, Mental, Emotional, and Physical, teaches us to deal with our thoughts, feelings, and actions in a mindful and mature manner.

When Berit started writing this book she made contact with the students that she had described in her first book EVERY CHILD HAS SPECIFIC NEEDS (2001). For this book UNDERSTANDING DIVERSITY (published in Swedish in 2015), Berit interviewed the same students and listened to their experiences some ten years later. She asked the students to tell her how they viewed their own development to mature and become adults.

The Waypoint Foundation, a not-for-profit center for educational development, is pleased to embrace the English translation of Berit Bergström's book UNDERSTANDING DIVERSITY. Janet Campbell and I, both representing The Waypoint Foundation, have assisted in moving this book forward beyond a Google translation. It has been a joy. And we are grateful to Cori Convertito for the book design.

Clarice M Yentsch, President
The Waypoint Foundation
36 Bahama Avenue, Key Largo, FL 33037   THE WAYPOINT FOUNDATION

PREFACE

For more than 40 years I have worked in the Swedish school system as a classroom teacher, special education teacher, and school leader/principal. Over this time, the schools' political and educational objectives and content have changed, and different curricula have been introduced. It started with a centrally-controlled school with given rules and standards. All of the students were expected to work in the same way. The teaching material was the same in all schools, and it was decided centrally which textbooks should be used. There were daily lesson plans to follow for the academic year. From there the development of a targeted school emerged, where the goal of the curriculum and the guidelines required individual plans with different learning materials available. Each teacher or team was to determine what was to be considered the best plan of work.

The school is a reflection of a rapidly changing society. The school was subject to change according to political control. Today I feel that there is no policy, and yet teachers are zealously required to evaluate the formal knowledge by documenting, evaluating, and assessing everything. Of course, it is important to have evaluations and documentation, but it must not be at the expense of the educational work, the teacher's own learning and creative preparation. The joy of being a teacher began to disappear.

There are many testimonials from teachers that they can no longer cope with this way of working. One may ask: Is it really through the control and weekly evaluations that we get an assessment of the students' knowledge? This work takes several hours per week of the teacher's pedagogical planning time. Does it not show that the documentation hysteria gives less time for us to be able to teach our students? For me, it has always been that the planning of the education work should come first. Getting the time to create the conditions for and commitment to each student's learning helps me give the student self-awareness, self-confidence, and the security they need in their learning. Good results are the effect of good pedagogy.

What skills are important to give our students? How can we best address them and provide the skills they will need in their future lives? Regardless of the curriculum, we need to be able to convey knowledge in several different ways. Since our students have different ways to learn, solve problems, and communicate, this is something we teachers must put in the center of our efforts. How do we teach the best way to create motivation and commitment? There are studies that show that the brain's passivity is greatest when they have long moments to sit and listen to someone talk without giving room for dialogue and participation. The interaction between teacher and student must be the foundation for lifelong learning. Researchers Vygotsky (1999), Dunn and Dunn (1992), Gardner (1991, 1993) and Vos and Dryden (1999) have for many years emphasized this.

As for myself, I came in contact with the psychologists Sandra Seagal and David Horne in the mid-1980s. Their work became for me the road leading to consciously meeting my students' various needs in their learning processes. This book is about my practical applications of their theories.

Thanks to you Simon, my oldest grandson, because you asked me: "Grandma, you need to write about how we are and how we learn. It has helped me so much, and I want to tell my friends. But it is not so easy to explain. It would be great if you could write more about it. And say that Simon's desires inspired you to write this book."

Finally, I thank Ulla Lindberg, former publisher at Runa Publishing Firm, for her editorial assistance, and Maria Renmyr who contributed many valuable comments during my writing. I also want to thank Clarice Yentsch and Janet Campbell for the great work they have done with the translation and editing of the English version of the book and for all the support they provided.

Stockholm 2017
Berit Bergström

INTRODUCTION

The purpose of this book is to give you a tool to gain a greater awareness of both yourself and others. The idea is that you should be able to use its content in the different stages of life. You may be surprised by how interesting meetings with people can become – with people who are completely different than yourself – once you appreciate the various ways of learning and communicating. It can be an exciting journey of self-discovery where you widen your vision and expand your first impression for why you are who you are and why you do what you do. This also gives you a deeper understanding of why others act as they do.

This book can be read in several ways. Some will immediately ask the question: "What is the purpose of the book?" Others do not care so much about finding out the purpose immediately, for it will certainly become evident. Still others will pretty quickly read it and even skim over certain areas, while others want to catch every word. Some will focus on the more personal and others are most interested in the facts. It may even be that once you read the content, its message may be perceived quite differently. Why is this?

It depends, of course, on the fact that we are all different. We experience the world around us in different ways. Different things are important to us, and we have different needs and different abilities. We live in different environments and cultures that influence our personality. What do we inherit and what is its impact? Scientists now agree that the viewpoint held in the 60s and 70s, that "we are largely influenced by the environment and less so by heritage" is no longer valid. Our environment and the people around us greatly influence us, but heritage is very important. Today, scientists believe that, already in the womb, we have an innate personality that will be with us throughout our life.

All cultures and societies create patterns, standards, and values. To become a part of our own culture, we adapt. Some can do this easily, whereas for others it is more difficult. If we can meet ambient values in a good way, blend into a context that is the norm, we often are treated positively. Already in kindergarten, children can be seen that easily adapt to the demands of society. They are the "easy" social children. There are also children whom we regard as odd because they do not easily crack the social code. These are children that we adults experience as having "problems". We do not understand them, and we judge them by our own values and experiences. The following little story shows how different we can interpret our surroundings and how it can create misunderstandings and negative thoughts about others.

It was time to choose a theme for the big project to work with during part of the last semester in grade 9. The overall task became: "Is the Earth a safe place to live?" The task had different subthemes to choose from: Earth's environment, Earth's resources, Man-Earth saviors or destroyers, new innovations.

In one group, Jonas was one of six participants. When the group first read through the instructions of the theme (note: written instructions), they

2

quickly began to debate the subthemes that could be most interesting for them. Some were quick to be heard. Axel threw himself into the conversation with enthusiasm, and even though he had few facts, he quickly brought up many thoughts and ideas to the others in the group.

He seemed so sure of what he said, Jonas became really jealous. "Axel always knows what he wants to do, does he not think? Am I the one who is slow-witted or what?" When Axel started throwing out ideas, there were those who caught on while it became quite messy and difficult for others to follow. For Jonas, who at the beginning of the task most wanted to sit quietly and listen to what the others came up with, this moment became stressful. He wanted to get the chance to think and be able to ask more questions, get more background, get more facts about the different subthemes. He was keen to get an overall picture of the expected outcome. He needed time to think and process through the task at hand, and he needed quiet to be able to contribute his views. He tried several times to enter the conversation with a question about where they could get more facts, but it seemed as if no one heard him. It ended up that he went silent and seemingly passive. Jonas looked around the group and saw that it seemed to be the same way for Erik. He had even turned away from the group and started to flip through some magazines. Jonas saw and judged Axel as a wiseacre who thought he knew everything. Axel in turn checked into the group and began to feel somewhat annoyed at Jonas and Erik and their seeming disinterest and passivity. "Why is it always me who has to pull the wagon when we're doing something?"

How often do we evaluate and judge others from our own frame of reference and our own way of being? Axel's need to quickly begin the task was interpreted by others that he seemed to know everything. He wanted to take power and run over the others, when it was really all about his eagerness to get going. By exchanging ideas and discussing with others, he pushed the work

3

forward. Jonas and Erik were more thoughtful and needed concrete facts and an opportunity to think in peace and quiet. It always took some time for them to come up with their contributions. This inaction Axel incorrectly interpreted as passivity and lack of interest.

WE THINK, FEEL, AND ACT

When we think, feel, and act, we do so in different ways. If, for example, we are asked to solve a task, some of us start in a structured and fact-oriented manner. Many others start in a more feeling and associative way. For still others, it is important that at the beginning of a task they understand and can visualize the practical benefits and get all the information they can before starting the task.

In 1979, Sandra Seagal began her work to try to understand what she calls the various basic processes or "Human Dynamics." In her work as a psychologist and psychotherapist, she could discern clear "patterns" of behavior in the people she met in the way they communicate, learn, and solve problems. She claimed to hear different patterns in their voices and speech patterns. She said that it seemed as if we have our own interplay between three basic elements active within us. The interaction of these components is the driving force of our actions. The three basic elements she termed as the Mental, Emotional, and Physical principles. The interaction among them and the degree of development of each comprise important parts of our way of being. All three parts have the same value and are needed for a life in balance. This forms the basis of Human Dynamics Theory.

> "These are basic threads in the human system, so fundamental and universal that we have termed them

principles. However well or poorly expressed, we see the mental, emotional and physical principles active in everyone." (Seagal and Horne, 1997, p. 23).

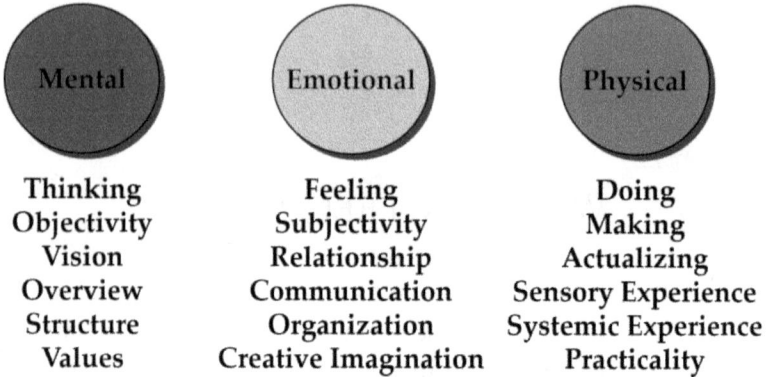

Mental	Emotional	Physical
Thinking	Feeling	Doing
Objectivity	Subjectivity	Making
Vision	Relationship	Actualizing
Overview	Communication	Sensory Experience
Structure	Organization	Systemic Experience
Values	Creative Imagination	Practicality

Through the Mental principle, we express our thoughts. It gives us the ability to see the value of an idea. It helps us to focus on a task, create structures and perspective, and define our values.

The Emotional principle is important in our interactions with others. It gives us the opportunity to subjectively feel and evaluate the sensitivity within ourselves and others. It helps us to organize, make connections, and create new forms. It is also important for our creative imagination.

The Physical principle is the implementation and practical part of us. It helps us to reconcile what to do and how to do it. It helps us to evaluate quality, function, and act holistically.

If a principle takes precedence over the other two, the natural interaction between the Mental, Emotional and Physical principles is disrupted, and we will be out of balance. That is what happened to Anna, Andreas, and Olle in the following stories.

Anna felt stressed. Today was a day when everything went wrong. First, she had overslept and missed the bus and arrived late for school and late for an important meeting that she was to attend. She had knocked over her milk on her new jeans and everything just malfunctioned. She found it difficult to collect her thoughts, and hard to keep focused on the task. Her thoughts went back and forth. It was as if her ability to think clearly had disappeared, that her feelings had completely taken over.

As she put the key in the door upon returning home and entered the hallway, she said to herself: "What awful luck I have had today. Why did this happen?" With a cup of tea, she sat at the kitchen table, and now she could just let the thoughts come, and the anxiety she felt all day began to drop away. She said to herself: "The next time it happens that things are like this, so wrong, I will not let myself get stressed out and will remember to take a few deep breaths. I will try to relax instead of being so tense."

When the day started so wrong for Anna, her emotions took command. Anna's three principles were not balanced. It turned out that the Mental principle retreated. As unrest spread within her, it got increasingly difficult for her to think clearly. As the Mental principle receded, she had difficulty focusing on a task, and she was not clear in her communication.

Although Andreas may now understand why it is important to work with others, as a young lad he did not understand. He was quite satisfied being by himself and consumed by his own thoughts. When someone started talking in a committed way, everything he experienced seemed like "emotional fuss", something he did not hear or understand. What others had to say he experienced as uninteresting, and he listened in a not-so-careful manner to what was being said. He lived very much in his own world, and when others did not agree, he removed himself and went his own way.

If for some reason the Emotional principle is not in balance with the other two principles, we have difficulty expressing emotions. One's own desires and needs are at the center. Having a judgmental attitude, Andreas had poor relations with the others. Had his Emotional principle been more involved with his Physical and Mental principles, he would have been able to see the value of the thoughts and feelings of others.

Another young male, Olle, always has many ideas when he goes to solve problems. With great intensity, strength, and joy, he takes on the task. He thinks and talks with others about his ideas. His workmates listen and think many times that his ideas are both interesting and exciting. But he does not go beyond the idea stage. Although he is passionate about the ideas, it seems that he does not have the capacity to implement them. It is often just words and thoughts. The danger is that the others look at Olle as a person who is just talk and not someone they can really rely on.

Olle's Physical principle needs to be trained so that he finds ways to implement his ideas. When his three principles are not interactive, he has difficulty bringing an idea to a practical implementation.

Mentally Centered	Emotionally Centered	Physically Centered

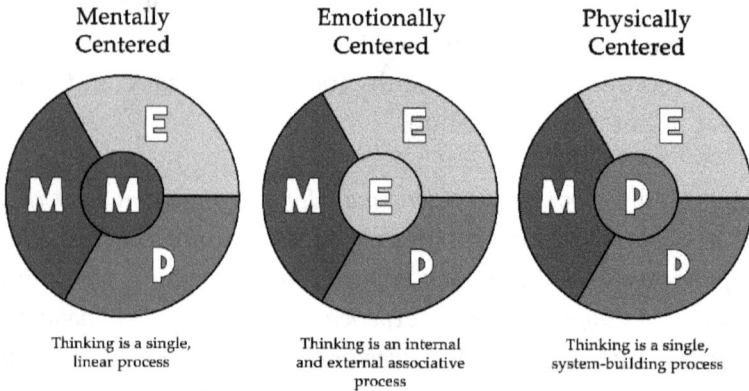

Thinking is a single, linear process	Thinking is an internal and external associative process	Thinking is a single, system-building process

The three principles have a dynamic interplay within us. It seems that one of them has a more central location and is the starting place for us. Depending on who I am, I start my process either based on my Mental, Emotional or Physical principle. You could call this the leading point of a thought or action.

To try to find out your centering, you may ask: "How do I address my information? What is my first reaction to an initiative, a problem, or a mission?" For most of us it is an unconscious and spontaneous reaction. When a problem has to be solved, it activates the centering and automatically starts the interaction with the other principles. We can be Mentally centered, Emotionally centered, or Physically centered. Out from this centering flows both the other two principles and the centered principle.

My friend Lennart was working as principal in a large secondary school outside of Stockholm. He believes he has a Mental centering, something he concluded based on the book on Human Dynamics Theory and in conversations with me. He prefers to start a task with written and fact-based information and wants to be able to process before he goes into some form of conversation and cooperation with others.

The verbal information he gives his colleagues and students is often of an overview character. For some of his associates, the information may be too sketchy. An example of this was when he explained the decision to move some of the classes in the school to a building nearby the school. Without adding any personal issues to the written statement, he informed his colleagues objectively why some classes had to move and what he had decided. The written information in which he informed his colleagues stated that more details would come later in the week.

In solving a problem, the Mentally centered individual attempts to solve the problem in a factual and objective way. Processing of the problem is done in a precise and linear fashion. With this linear way, I mean that the person's thoughts lay out like "rails" and are followed without slipping onto some "side track". To collect, understand, and draw conclusions, everything follows logically from one point to another. Thinking is an internal process. You think first and then you speak. The words are often carefully chosen and are precise and accurate.

Alva became thoughtful. Some days after the meeting with Lennard the leaflet lay in her compartment. In the leaflet, there was nothing of what the team had discussed. It was just about the two classes that had to move. Alva and Lena had objected very clearly that it was unfair and should not happen. The students "banished away" from school would come to feel left out. Work would be more difficult for both teachers and students, and Alva had told Lennart about her past experiences from a workplace she had been part of before. There, they had done exactly what he planned to do, and it had not been good. Why was Lennart not inviting and listening to the staff experience? She must talk with Lena about this.

Unlike Lennart, both Alva and Lena self-identified to have an Emotional centering. Emotionally centered people relate a task or problem to their own personal experiences and life events, and process more associatively. They often have an inner dialogue or are in conversation with others. Problem solving is affected by the situation the person is in and what others have to say about the matter. Talk and mind go hand-in-hand, and talking about a subject clarifies their own thinking.

Carl, self-identified as having a Physical centering, sat quietly during the meeting. He did not yet know what he would think. For him, the information had been too brief and he had many questions. He would have liked more background information and wondered why Lennart suggested the solution that he did. In a longer perspective, what was the reason for the school to make this change? When Alva asked him what he thought, it was difficult to give her an answer. He must first calmly get the opportunity to think through the whole thing again and get the whole picture. His own team would be split up. What would this lead to and what were the practical implications?

For one who is Physically centered, the process starts with collecting relevant facts and past experiences. The person's quest for concrete understanding and an overall view of the task is a very important part of the process. If Physically centered, you do not act until the whole picture is clear. You want to be in concert with others to solve a problem in a practical and effective manner. Thinking is, as for the Mentally centered, an internal process, and you need to think before you speak.

In reviewing the different ways of reacting to the information that their headmaster gave, consider: What could Lennart have done, as the leader, to better accommodate the different needs of the staff? Like most issues, he presented his information in the way that suited him and was not thinking about how the information would be received differently. Had he been more aware of the different centerings of his staff, he would have given Alva more space to discuss and express views. He would then realize how her thoughts, feelings, and speech are closely connected and how she related to what he said. If the group had been given the information before the meeting, Carl could more fully understand the implications of what Lennart intended and then become more active in subsequent discussions.

Five basic processes

There is a close connection between the centering principle and one of the other principles. We tend to talk about personal basic patterns, when describing this relationship. You could instead use the concept of processes. This is to clarify that this is something that can be diverse and more dynamic than a pattern, which can be perceived to be more static. To further illustrate, I give the following examples:

Mental-physical (Mp)

For those who have the Mental-physical process, the information is processed in a linear, logical, selective, and detached way. The person often acts on the basis of what is perceived valuable and with connections to strong values that have a central place in what is done or should be done.

Emotional-mental (Em)

For those who have the Emotional-mental process, ideas and feelings are closely linked. Ideas are processed in an associative and spontaneous way, often in communication with others. If it is meaningful for the person, new ideas and future visions of creative work become apparent.

Emotional-physical (Ep)

If a person has the Emotional-physical process, the Emotional centering is closely linked to the Physical part. Interaction between the two principles is manifested in the reaction of the person to his/her environment. This too is in a spontaneous, non-linear way. Moods and emotions of others are easily picked up and related to oneself.

Physical-mental (Pm)

A person who has the Physical-mental process addresses ideas and facts in a practical, systematic, and system-oriented manner. The aim is to create efficient and effective systems. Step-by-step, a structure becomes created and leads to solving a problem or task.

Physical-emotional (Pe)

For people with the Physical-emotional process, the task treats the complex relationship between people, actions, and events in a practical and systems-oriented manner. By processing a large amount of data and details, an overall picture emerges.

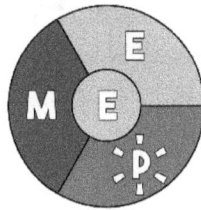

Mental-Physical   Emotional-Mental   Physical-Mental

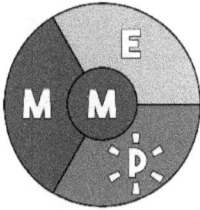

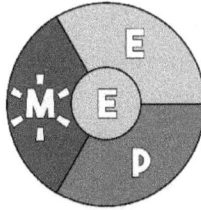

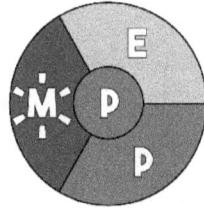

Emotional-Physical   Physical-Emotional

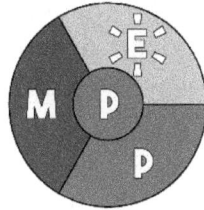

The three principles, (Mental, Emotional, Physical) can shape nine different combinations. From experience to date with western cultures, the five combinations described above are most frequently encountered. After thousands of interviews from various studies, observations, and video footage, deep and comprehensive knowledge of each of the five basic processes has been gained.

On the following pages, you will get to meet people who self-identified to each of the five most frequently encountered processes. They will describe their different ways of working and the needs they have when it comes specifically to communication, learning, and development.

Before that, we must ask: "But where is the third principle?" We have already talked about a dynamic interplay between the Mental, Emotional and Physical components. These are manifested as primary, secondary, and tertiary. When the knowledge of one's basic processes becomes clear, one can more consciously develop the third principle and its interaction with the other two. The third principle plays a very special part, which is described later in this book.

Although every human being is unique, there are fundamental similarities in people with the same basic process as to learning, problem solving, and communication. Even the gathering of information and how frequently various words are used in communication can be indicative. People with the same basic processes can, however, be very different in their behavior. Behavior is formed by the culture and the environment. The behavior arises from ambient expectations and the norms and values that apply in the community. Another difference between two individuals with the same basic process can be linked to the quantitative distribution of the principles and how well the principles are integrated.

One of the most important things to understand is that there is no difference in value between the different basic processes. One is not better than the others. It is not that a person with a specific process is smarter, more intelligent, or more mature than a person with another process. We all have our qualities and abilities that can be developed if we get the opportunity to be who we truly are and get our specific needs met.

PERSONAL STORIES

After more than 35 years in the world of schools, I wrote my first book EVERY CHILD HAS SPECIFIC NEEDS (2001). It was about my students' different ways of being and learning. Meeting with the students and trying to understand their way of learning was like a puzzle, where the pieces began to fall into place one by one. After a number of months with my new knowledge based on Human Dynamics Theory, I was able to see and understand the students' different basic processes more and more. The most important thing for me was to consciously create a safe environment for all students and to meet their various needs in the learning situation.

When I started writing this book, I made contact with the students that I had described in the first book. I had let them take part in the various descriptions of their way of functioning in my first book. For this book, I interviewed them and listened to their experiences, some ten years later. I asked them to tell me about the way they communicate and how they viewed their own development to become adults.

Simon -- The Emotional-physical process

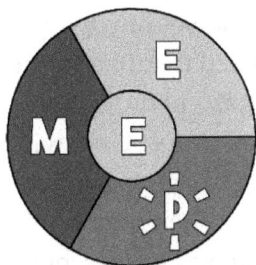

Simon is now 20 and studying at a college. He says it is very easy for him to pick up the signals that surround him in his environment. This applies to both his own feelings and the feelings of others. He describes what he perceives, e.g. as wordless communication, or concern for the group. Sometimes this means that he has difficulty concentrating on the task at hand.

As a child, it was very important for him to feel accepted and popular and to obtain confirmation from others. He explained "Many times I asked my parents if what I made or wrote was good enough. Did they think it was good? When I got a positive response from them, I felt calmer. Not that I need direct confirmation from them today, but it really does feel good when their positive response comes. Today confirmation from others is not as important as it was when I was younger. It was pretty hard to absorb everything and all the time be dependent on what others thought and think about me. Now I have gotten better at valuing things without being influenced by others and may instead ask whether there is any reason to care about or be affected by this."

With Simon, always the emotion is in the center when he is faced with a decision. He says, "When I follow my feelings, there is often a good outcome, but they should not take over. It is easy to get carried away emotionally, and then I have to say to myself 'Simon, you need to think clearly and analyze the issue.' It can be difficult to distinguish between things and people, and it is easy to take on other people's feelings and problems and become consumed by them."

If a task is unclear, Simon can feel a concern that causes him to have difficulty sitting still. He feels restless and may need to move about. The lack of clarity makes him talk more than usual – in order to put words into his thoughts. Today if something is unresolved with another person, he will ask, "What is this I feel? Something does not feel good between us. Can we talk about it?" When Simon told me this, I thought about what happened when he was in preschool. It shows the sensitivity of people with an Emotional-physical process and the concerns that arise when one does not understand other peoples' signals.

When Simon had completed almost the entire first semester in preschool, he said several times. "I do not want to go to the preschool, and I do not like to make the rabbit. It is not fun." The rabbit came up several times. Simon's mother was in contact with the preschool teacher. She understood that rabbits represented something that Simon could not explain. In the conversation with his teacher, the mother asked if anything happened or what the rabbit could possibly stand for. The teacher said she feels great irritation that Simon takes so much time and space in the group of children, that he is so restless and cannot sit still during group exercises. His mother asked if she had talked with Simon about this irritation. His teacher replied that she had done this several times. It had been when the children were sitting in the group, but not directly in private conversation with Simon.

Simon's mother then suggested a talk with Simon, the teacher, and herself. The teacher explained her annoyance about the fact that Simon took so much space and that the other children were often interrupted by him when they were trying to tell something. Simon became influenced by the teacher's negative feelings, and it meant that he talked a lot more than usual and could not sit still. When he did not understand and picked up the teacher's irritation, it created a concern in him. Then Simon and the teacher agreed upon a secret language. When the teacher thought that Simon took up too much space in the group, she made an agreed-upon sign that Simon knew. With that, he felt satisfied and happy, "rabbits" were no longer a problem.

But back to what Simon now says many years later. He believes that people who do not talk as much as he does could experience him as quite demanding. "I talk to create a community where everyone should feel that they have an opportunity to influence and be involved. It is important for me to have a good dialogue, but I should perhaps think more about inviting those who often sit silent and give them more space to be heard." One thing that he had noticed was that many of his pals would not dare show their feelings. It may be important to them to act tough in front of others, and not be seen as sentimental. He says: "My parents have understood how important my feelings are and how I react upon them. So you could say, I was lucky."

In recent years, Simon has a greater ability to keep things at a distance and be more objective. He can be more selective in what he does and does not get involved in. About his future, he says: "A positive environment where I feel that I am accepted, loved, and needed will always be important for me. When my friends and my family are doing well, and we have fun together, then I also feel good. When emotions are allowed to flow – then it is bloody funny. I want to live fully and have many happy memories until I die."

Young Simon wanted to satisfy his parents, teachers and friends all the time. Today he does not need their confirmation in the same way as earlier. He may find it difficult to say no and takes part in or organizes too many different things. Then he can become tired and a bit angry and annoyed. "Why can't someone else take responsibility? Should it always be me to get involved?"

If you have the Emotional-physical process, you can easily become a victim of the circumstances. In stressful situations, people with this process can easily become unfocused and have difficulty getting things done. It feels as if everything just gets messy. Then they might respond with a stomach ache or headache. In the story of Simon and pre-school, he became stressed and sad when he did not understand what was wrong, and he became chatty. Everything was hard and uncomfortable, and he just wanted to get away from it.

Everyone has specific qualities and abilities, and people with the Emotional-physical process have a tendency to easily put themselves into other people's thoughts and feelings. Thereby they often create positive sentiments in a group and try to make sure everyone's needs are met. The variety allows for many creative ideas. There is also an ability to organize and see the connection between people and things.

The story of Tommy, another student with the Emotional-physical process

Tommy was in my class in sixth grade. Every morning when I came to school, he stood outside the classroom door and waited. For him it was very important to have personal contact with me. Just a few words to show my interest in him would make the day begin well. I could say, for example, "What nice shoes you have. Are they new?" or "How was it at football practice yesterday?" Before the tests in English and mathematics, Tommy would feel very restless and totally lose his focus. He had trouble sitting still, and he would run out to the bathroom several times. I sat down next to him to calm him and would say, "Close your eyes and take some deep breaths. Sit for a while and feel your breathing, and a calmness will spread in your body, and you can start with your task."

There is a sensitivity to how other people are talking. It may be, for example, when you need help with solving a task. Because you always are sensitive to ambient ways of relating, you can be blocked and go in defense, especially if a person is talking to you in an irritated or harsh tone. Multi-focus makes it easy to take in the environment, and then it can be difficult to keep focus on just one or a few things. With too much going on, you might need help choosing from the diversity of things to do.

Amanda -- The Emotional-mental process

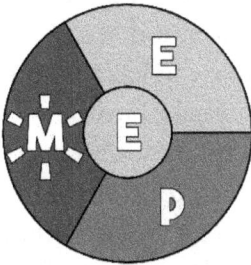

Amanda is now 17 years old, with many activities and friends and intense days. One of her main interests is gymnastics where she competes at the elite level. She has just started her last year of high school.

She recognizes much of the description of the Emotional-mental process, even if she believes that she has changed a lot since she was little. Previously, it was difficult for her to summarize and finish a task in school. She got tired before it was finished and would have liked to start with something new to do. Now she says that completing what she is doing is something she learned. To be involved in a task and be able to influence decisions is important for Amanda. Actually, it is not that she wants to make the decision, rather more to be involved and come up with new ideas. She says "If nobody grabs what should be done, I will be the one who starts the task." She feels that she has learned to be more patient and let others participate and invite them to say what they think, not just be the one who forces her ideas.

It is important for her to get started, such as when she has an idea. One example she gave is when the family planned their midsummer holiday. "Directly when we started talking about it, I got more ideas on what we could do. I started talking about them and got a little impatient when everyone came with their comments and suggestions. I wanted simply to decide about what to do and we could adjust the details later. I wanted to get started right away, and when I get an idea, I immediately want to tell it to others."

Sometimes Amanda gets anxious, though it soon passes. An example of this can be when people change what they decided. On her gymnastics team, there are many strong wills, and discussions can sometimes be lively. Amanda says she thinks she has become better at listening to others, for example, in discussing how to add up the group's various programs. Quite right, she knows how she wants it, but says "Then I take a deep breath and try to wait out the others." She feels that she has learned to say things in a different way than before. She is more cautious and gentle as she moves forward, especially when she is talking to those she knows could be hurt if she is too direct in communication with them.

"One of my problems is that I have such a bad memory" she says. When her friends tell their memories of different events, she will not remember what they are talking about. She just remembers what for her was most essential, not all the things surrounding that. She thinks that it can sometimes be difficult like when her grandmother asked "Amanda, do you remember when you last had a day off from school, and we saw the movie together?" and she had to answer "No, what movie was it?" She went on to say, "Grandma seems to remember everything. Maybe she will be sorry that I do not remember, but I cannot help it."

Justice and fair play are values that are deep and important for her. She reacts strongly when she experiences something unfair and unjust. Then she must speak out as clearly as possible. It can then happen that someone feels hurt, but she just has to. "For me, my family is very important. Family is where I can come and feel safe and be who I am. Sometimes it is close friends where I can feel safe and be who I am. Just to feel safe with the people that are around me, to be able to talk about my problems and get advice is important. There are those in the school who are constantly playing a role and cannot be themselves. They probably feel very insecure with who they are."

When I asked how she sees the future, Amanda responded: "I have nothing planned for the future. It may come to me. I am open to a broad education and can then decide on my way. The future will only come as it comes. One thing I know that I will do is to vote and make my voice heard. It is wrong not to do so. I have a voice, and I can affect things. Nobody can do everything – but everyone can do something."

Amanda says that ideas come so fast, and she immediately wants to get out and act on what it is, such as in the planning of the Midsummer celebrations and programs for her gymnastics team. She becomes frustrated by not getting started fast enough, and sometimes she can seem to be tough, which is her drive forward, not because she desires to run over anyone. It may be something that is good for the rest of us to know. It is sometimes difficult to interpret her facial expression and body language and understand how she really feels. The following event is an example of how Amanda behaved in school in grade 3.

During the break, Amanda and two other girls were fighting with each other. When they came back into the classroom, the teachers asked what had happened. The two other girls were very upset and crying, while Amanda sat quietly and watched them without showing any of her own emotions. The teacher wondered if Amanda also was sad about what had happened, or maybe it was that she did not care. On that, Amanda replied: "Camilla and Jenny cry with their eyes, but I cry in my heart."

When the Emotional-mental child has experienced anything outrageous, unfair, or sad, the reaction to the incident often comes much later. Something of what had happened during the day can make the child very angry at the dinner table, and he/she starts to argue and yell about something else not connected at all to the event earlier in the day. As an adult, you then can ask the child whether something special happened during the day. Then the whole story comes out, and there is an explanation as to why he/she feels so bad. Then you get the opportunity to go back to the event and talk about it.

People with this Emotional-mental process see a challenge in what can be created. They like to exchange ideas with others, to associate freely and come up with new ideas, motivate, and create engagement. Changes are both exciting and challenging when opportunities come forward. The activities are mostly directed outward and forward, and the person does not notice that he/she can be both hungry and tired. The whole time, focus is on what will happen and what should be done. When solving a task, the person wants to start the task with little background information, and can be irritated by getting too many details in the beginning that for the moment are considered unnecessary. Ideally, he/she wants to start working and then absorb more of the information and details when needed. If there is structure in a task in an early stage, there can be great flexibility allowing the structure to be changed during the work. Some have likened the Emotional-mental process to a sailboat sailing toward a jetty. Depending on the wind, the person can steer in a new direction several times before ending up at the jetty. People with this process see the possibilities of new ideas. They are innovators and dare to be risk-takers. They have creative ideas, are problem solvers, and lead the group forward in a responsible manner.

Jenny – the Physical-emotional process

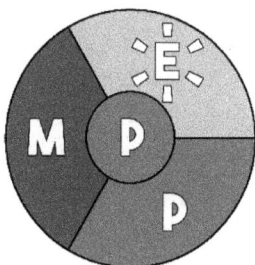

Jenny was one of my students in grades 4-6. Several years later after I left that school, I contacted her and asked if she wanted to read and comment on the story I wrote in my first book about students' basic patterns. At first, she was quite doubtful. She needed to get detailed information about the purpose of the interview I wanted to do and what it was all about. Once she read her story, she thought that she had a better and clearer picture of what was expected of her.

Jenny began by saying that she needed some background as to what she should do. "I need to have the historical perspective, knowing what happened in the past, as well as coherence and a form of whole to understand the task. In my studies, it is sometimes difficult when I only get fragments, parts of that I will learn. Then I will not understand. When I read something, all the words have the same value, and I find it difficult to pull out what is most essential from the text, because I think everything is important." In Jenny's further comments, she said that it seems she sees and feels a lot more than what most others do.

She feels as though her senses are stronger than others. When she looks at one thing, it can be a beautiful dish, a table, a fabric, or something else, she wants to see both the shape of the object, feel the texture of the material, smell it, almost taste it, to really know what it is. She thinks she has a good memory, especially when it comes to events or decisions she has been involved in. She can still give details of the Vikings' voyages to the East, a group effort in grade 4 that she found fun and interesting.

She went on to say: "*As I take in so much I do need to be alone and sort out my thoughts. Something I constantly struggle with is to not be so detailed. Sometimes it feels as if it just becomes too much. It is as if I have small compartments in the brain when I sort out my thoughts. I can become stressed, but I do not think others experience this because I often hear 'Oh Jenny, it's so nice with you, you are always so calm and safe.' This happens even if my insides feel like the ocean in a storm.*"

People with this Physical-emotional process want to start their task with an open mind and experience being in the middle of the situation. They take in all of the information and knowledge without first selecting, sorting out, or structuring. There may be a large amount of data to be processed. The structure reveals itself rather late in the processing of what the person has as a task. The details of the mass of facts must be linked to previous experience and knowledge in order to be able to understand. Old knowledge brings new knowledge.

When Jenny is able to be careful, detailed, and precise, without feeling stressed or pressured, she feels satisfied. The good memory she talks about is something many other persons with Physical-emotional process also talk about. Even if it has been many years ago, one can describe an event in great detail. Being trustworthy is important, and they say nothing if they do not know for sure what to think of an issue. It can be annoying when people come with claims that are not substantiated or when a person is constantly changing position. If the image is not ready, they will ask some questions, since it is very important that whatever they say and do is right and proper.

For Jenny, it can be a stress factor when she does not get to finish what she was doing. When that happens or when too much is going on in the surrounding environment, she says that it feels like chaos in her brain, and she has difficulty taking in information. Another stress factor is when she must make a decision too quickly, when she feels like she does not have time to think it through. For her, it is important to be allowed to speak to the point and offer her own opinions without being interrupted.

The Physical-emotional process allows them to connect to themselves and assume their own personal thoughts, ideas, and experiences. When they agree with something said in a group, there is no need to repeat the opinion. There is no great need to "prove" verbally, but this can lead to misunderstandings. Others may think that they are not interested or that they do not have an opinion about what is being discussed. A person with the Physical-emotional process may be interested and have opinions. Or he/she might need to bring in relevant comments, weigh the pros and cons, and take time to think through where one stands to provide a credible and correct response.

People with the Physical-emotional process have the ability to ensure the practical utility of a task, and they have a good memory. Often people with this process are good listeners. They listen to everything that is said, all the details that come up, and take in various moods and others' experiences. Usually this is done in a calm manner and with an even temper. The few times that a Physical-emotional person gets angry, anger can be expressed in an explosion of words and emotions.

Malin – the Physical-mental process

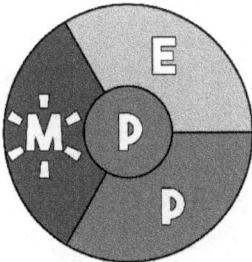

Malin was a female student in a colleague's class and, since our classes cooperated often, I got to know Malin well. Today, Malin, 20, is studying economics at a university. When Malin read the story of her process, she thought that much of it was true, but also believes that a lot comes from her own development. She still lays out plans and makes lists of everything she should do, regarding it as the most efficient way. When she was little, she planned everything, for example, her routines that she must follow every morning. She describes it this way: *"I got up, made the bed, got dressed, ate breakfast, watched TV, brushed my teeth, and then went to school." If she woke up too late and did not have time to make the bed. Then she thought she was not good. Today she is not so slavishly following her plans even if they are still very important to her. Now she can easily change them, yet it can sometimes irritate her if one thing does not go as she planned. She gives an example: "Last Saturday, I had planned to bake and just when I would begin, my sister came to visit. Then I felt really annoyed, she disrupted my plan, although I was happy to see her. But I train myself to try to be more flexible."*

Malin thinks she still has difficulty with "small talk". She calls this talk that leads nowhere. To just talk for talk's sake, she sees no value. However, if there is something she is interested in and committed to, she is quite talkative.

She says she is surprised when someone experiences her as "angry" or "sour" when she was just listening. Maybe she looks serious, and it is interpreted that she is not interested or disapproving. She would honestly say what she thinks if she does not agree with something. She would not agree just to make someone happy. In the past, she could not say that a friend's shirt is fine if she did not like it. Today she says instead: "It's a shirt for you, but it probably would not suit me."

She cannot stick with a task if she does not see a clear purpose. If the purpose of the task is unclear, she must create a purpose herself for what she should do. When something is unclear, she will ask questions to clarify it all. She says: "What I am interested in I want to learn everything, indeed digging all the way to China if necessary. But things that do not interest me, I can easily leave." This was evident when she got her first grades in high school. Some subjects she had the highest score in; other subjects she was not interested in, she received poor scores. "It was a wakeup call for me. I had to strain to create an interest for the topics that I did not like."

People with Physical-mental process, just as Malin says, need to know the purpose of a task before they can get to work. They also need to know the practical usefulness of the task and what is expected of them. They then can provide facts and data related to the purpose and add a timetable. It is constantly important to relate to the whole of the task and to work strategically and methodically against objectives. They are both systemic and systematic in their work. By that I mean, they work in a systematic manner in the context of a given task and assemble the parts into a whole system. For them, it is important to gain an understanding when solving problems. They find it a great help to have access to charts, maps, and models related to a task. They need peace and quiet to take their own time to interconnect the thoughts, the body, and the different rhythms of the surroundings.

Once the purpose of the task is clear, it is time to lay out the plan. They will gradually follow a preliminary plan which is then adjusted and refined. It comes to saving time, resources, and energy to achieve its objectives in the most effective way. Depending on how one values a task, it can be solved with a small amount of facts and information. A comprehensive and detailed plan evolves. When there is an engaging task, the person with a Physical-mental process wants to know everything, often with a keen interest in how things work, both theoretically and practically. When the focus is on a working task, the person can forget to take in the human aspect, to allow others to get involved. When Malin says her friends think she is "sour", it may be one such occasion. She listens quietly and is really committed and interested, but she is not aware of ambient signals and may forget to socially connect with others.

Something that might seem strange is that people with the Physical-mental process have two different rhythms. One is a rapid rhythm in the thoughts and a slower rhythm of speech and movement. If there is an imbalance between these two rhythms, the person can feel stressed and irritable. It is important to help the Physical-mental person to become aware of his/her two rhythms and listen to the signals, both physical and emotional.

Dominant qualities in people with this Physical-mental process are the precision and accuracy with which data and tasks are performed. Preconceptions of what should be done and planning contribute to effective work. Just as with the Emotional-mental people, one strives to be a problem solver. Physical-mental individuals are also good listeners who often give unconditional support to those who need assistance. The ability for three-dimensional vision and spatial intelligence can be strengths of this person.

Gustav – the Mental-physical process

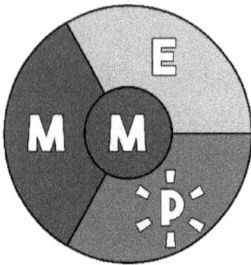

Gustav was introduced in my description of the Mental-physical process. As of this writing, he is 15 years old and in high school. Based on the description of the Mental-physical process, and after he read the story of how as a child he did not want to play in the "ballsea" that was on a Mac Donald's restaurant play area, he made some comments. In the restaurant's play corner, he did not join together with the other children, but said he would wait until all the children had gone home. He wanted to be alone in the "ballsea". It was as if he wanted some distance from the others. Today he feels that he does not recognize this. He says: *"Of course I can swim and bathe in a pool, even though there are other people there that I do not know or have a relationship with. I may not have direct contact with anyone, but with my friends I can have fun and play."*

He always wants to check out the situation before he starts working on a task. *"For me it is important to know things in advance and do not throw me into the unknown. Sure, I can improvise a bit, but when it comes to new things, I would rather check carefully."* He generally prefers to be on the edge of a group; he does not need and does not want to be in the center. He says: *"I am with what the group is doing, without being in the middle."* He does not want to be close to people he does not know so well. *"My family, however, is very close to me."*

Gustav likes to work both individually and in groups. It is best to get the task first, to read it, and then discuss it in the group. But then the group should not be too large. It depends very much on the group composition as to whether or not he wants to go in and engage in a discussion. If there is someone who talks all of the time and takes much space, then he is silent. He cannot interrupt anyone, but if he gets space to be heard, he talks happily and puts forward his views. In a stressful situation, Gustav can react by becoming more enclosed in himself. This is often interpreted by others as dissociation.

Such a situation, for example, is when he is given a description of a task that is too vague or comprehensive. Gustav says several times that he learns most easily when the information is consistent with what he values and thinks is important. Perhaps he would "turn off", and not listen when the task he has is not particularly interesting. However, he has realized the importance of self-discipline. It may be that he is stuck in a task and sees the solution in only one way. Then he may need help to recognize that a problem can have several approaches and solutions.

Characteristic for persons with Mental-physical process is that they would prefer to start their task visually. By that I mean, they prefer to see and read about the task first, and later talk about it. In a structured, logical, focused and selective manner, they take in the facts/data when the task is presented. The parts are logically focused, and a comprehensive overall picture without too many curves emerges. Being in a task, they have no problem going from a macro to micro perspective or the reverse. They quickly adapt to changes of time and space scales.

An example of this was when Gustav's class would work with the environment as a theme. He began to consider the task in a macro perspective of the whole Earth and its resources. He posed the question: "How can I, as the little person that I am, help to create a better environment?" To answer, the next step was that he went down to the micro level and started to investigate how waste management was organized in his local municipality and put a proposal out to streamline it. At the end of the work, he again went up on a macro level and presented ideas about the influence of more efficient waste management in a global perspective.

As Gustav is so precise and meticulous, he wants to process and refine his data several times. When it comes to working with others, he does it usually in a small group or, as he says, he prefers to work alone. It happens that his communication is written, rather than verbal, in this way it becomes more clear and precise.

The Mental-physical person is often perceived by the outside world as stable and calm. Emotions have a steady stream inside and are often not visible. An exception might be if their own values are violated. In that instance, they will show both anger and other strong emotions. They are selective and choose with great care including the people they associate with.

The qualities that characterize people with Mental-physical process are the ability to view things objectively and to explain the value of different viewpoints. They are able to summarize what has been said in a group and account for results and to constantly maintain focus in a discussion. They are useful to a group when the discussion is divergent and results are perceived differently.

Seagal and Horne (1997) wrote that in their encounters with people, it is rare to find people who have the Mental-physical process. In all my years as a teacher, only a few students seemed to have this process. One of them was Henry who was a student in the second grade. Unaware of his needs and because of my inexperience at the time, I interpreted that Henry was a lonely child. He was difficult to reach, and one who had problems with his social development. He went mostly off by himself, had rare spontaneous contact with me or others, and, during breaks, he was always the boy who was on the periphery of the group. It made me concerned. I tried many times to "push" him to join the group when they were out playing in the yard. Then he would look at me very surprised and say "But I am in the group."

Another example comes to mind, and by this time I was more aware of our different ways of being and of our different needs. Erik, whose parents I knew well, was looking at me hesitantly when I came home to his family for a visit. Erik was watching me with his big blue eyes. Ideally, I would have liked to give him a really big hug, but I knew it was not appropriate. Not because of his age, but he just needed space around him. Although I wanted to hug him and lift him up onto my lap, I knew that he himself must make that choice, when it suited him. Given his natural distance and the space he needed around him, I knew that he would pull away if I became too intrusive. Big emotions were not something he appreciated. When everyone in his surroundings let him develop out from his own needs in peace and quiet, it created a fine interplay between him and those around him.

WE LEARN IN DIFFERENT WAYS

Albert Einstein has been described as a student who had trouble adjusting to the school's requirements. "One of his teachers once said to him: 'You will never amount to anything.' This hardly makes him seem a dazzling student." (B. Hoffman, p 20). Yet he became one of the world's top scientists. Winston Churchill was a "bad" school pupil; he stammered and lisped, but became a prominent leader, author, and speaker. And Thomas Alva Edison was considered to be a lively and animated child who asked too many questions. Today would people perhaps diagnose him as a child with ADHD? He could not go to his own school, but had to have homeschooling. He became one of the greatest inventors of all time. Could it be that Einstein, Churchill, and Edison had learning processes that do not match the education in their schools?

In the late 1970s, I began to wonder if the school could sometimes be an obstacle for some children's learning. How tragic. I had gifted students who had difficulties to follow mainstream education. Was it the student or the school system that failed when it could not accommodate the student's way of learning? What was it? Was I teaching in a way that did not correspond to their learning needs? During my years as a special education teacher, I became more and more aware of the importance of communication between me and the students. When I more consciously started listening to my students' different needs in learning, I got a greater understanding and could adapt my communication to them so that my words strengthened their learning. Communication and learning are close together. Good communication can be one important key to learning.

A researcher who has meant a lot to me and has been a guide of my work is Lev Vygotsky (1999), the Belarusian pedagogic researcher. He was recognized in the 1960s throughout the Western world for his theories of child development and learning. He thought that learning is not a solo performance nor a passive response. Both those who learn and those who teach are engaged in a social interaction. This is a prerequisite for learning and development to take place. Vygotsky saw human learning as a process, linked to a social nature, in which children grow into the intellectual life of the people around them. He also felt that the human way of being was related to the outside world during childhood and shaped by both biological and social conditions and characteristics. He had a dynamic view of the role of the teacher and what the teacher could do to help students in their learning processes.

Many other researchers have demonstrated the importance of communication for learning. Among other things, Lars Svedberg (2003) described it, from a constructivist perspective. He says that the understanding of himself and his environment is the starting point for learning. In order to understand others' learning processes, we must first understand our own. The understanding is needed both in theory and the analytical models and teaching methods. One can see it as crucial for the students' achievement.

C. Brook shows in her study, "The Circle of Learning, Learning Styles in Native Adult Educational Programs" (1987) how different the theoretical capacity can be to learn and solve specific sets of data. Participants in the study were 203 Native American women. She found that the women's cultural background, their way to communicate, and their different learning processes could be perceived as an obstacle. When the teacher did not reach the students in their communication, Brook felt that it was because the teacher had a different process than the students, and it created an obstacle in their learning.

When I got to know the different processes, I realized how blind and deaf I had been for the students who had learning processes and communication preferences other than my own! I thought that, if only I taught as well as I could, everyone would learn. But that is not so. I know today that I did not reach some students, and they had a hard time to understand and learn when I taught only from my own way of being.

When we encounter obstacles, we must stop and reflect on why we are not getting through. How often do we ask ourselves: "Can I introduce this subject in a different way? Have I given sufficient information and time for the students who need more time to think? Have I been sufficiently clear and complete in my description of the task and requests?"

Based on the three centerings, the Mental, the Emotional and the Physical, I have listed a few words to show what to consider in teaching students with these centerings. The different centerings' function, and the process is started and completed differently. This picture below gives a brief overview.

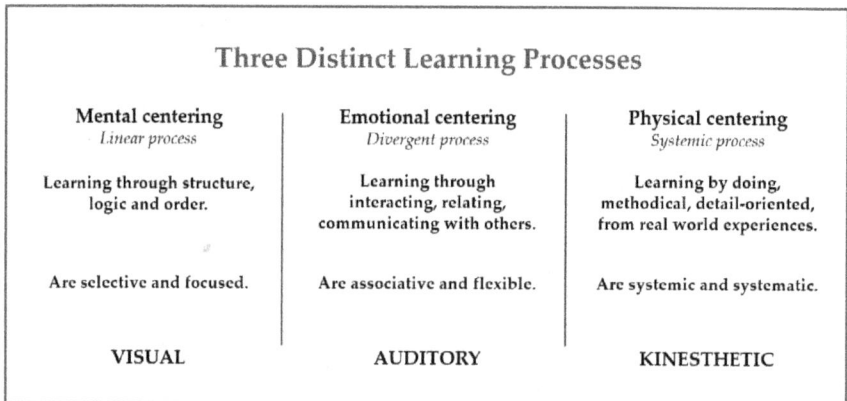

Three Distinct Learning Processes

Mental centering	Emotional centering	Physical centering
Linear process	*Divergent process*	*Systemic process*
Learning through structure, logic and order.	Learning through interacting, relating, communicating with others.	Learning by doing, methodical, detail-oriented, from real world experiences.
Are selective and focused.	Are associative and flexible.	Are systemic and systematic.
VISUAL	**AUDITORY**	**KINESTHETIC**

LEARNING PROCESSES

Basic learning processes depend on the different centerings. Here you will re-meet Simon, Amanda, Jenny, Malin, and Gustav, who will tell us about what is important for them in learning.

Emotionally centered learning processes

It starts with an auditory signal; you want first to hear and talk about what is to be learned. There is also an associative process with many personal touches. For those who have the Emotional-physical learning process, the link between the Emotional centering and the Physical part is clear. The teacher can link up with his/her own personal stories about the subject matter. It is important that good relations are maintained and that the learning environment provides an opportunity for creative expression. For those who have the Emotional-mental learning process, the Emotional centering is closely linked to the Mental part. The process also starts in an associative way with dialogue about ideas.

SIMON – AN EMOTIONAL-PHYSICAL LEARNING PROCESS

When I want to learn something, I begin to listen to what the teacher has to say about the task. I listen, take in the surroundings and detect if it feels good. When it feels good, then I continue to take in what I have to learn, and then it seems so simple. If I have a boring task which does not inspire me, I feel a resistance, and it becomes much more difficult. It has been very easy to connect to myself and to my own experiences. Just as it says in the first book, EVERY CHILD HAS SPECIFIC NEEDS, it is like I am starting to lay out a "puzzle" from the information that I get.

An example of this was when my classmate and I chose to do a musical paper, our special project in the third year of high school. We had a lot of puzzle pieces: layouts, graphics, pictures, and content, etc. All of the pieces were laid in front of us. Where would we start? We began by picking up a few pieces of the puzzle, and when some fit together nicely, we could put more and more pieces together.

The whole structure of the work came together, and we were excited when we saw how good it would be. It is good for me to know in advance how much time the job is expected to take. If I do not get a time frame, I can "bloom" out in several directions, and it can feel stressful to be ready in time.

Simon's learning process starts audibly; first he would like to listen to something. These may be facts, a story, or any event retold. He starts working with what he heard or read, and with things that feel personally relevant to him. He receives the task in a subjective manner, both personally and emotionally. If the contact with the teacher does not feel good, he can turn off his attention. Therefore, it is very important that he feels safe, accepted, and has a good relationship with his teachers.

The next step in the process is that Simon sees connections between the new material he has to handle and his earlier experiences. Past experience and the new knowledge can be likened to the "puzzle pieces" of which he speaks. At the beginning of the process, he may feel some anxiety and wonder if he will be able to learn the new information. Perhaps he begins to aimlessly "pick" the "pieces". He asks many questions and may be perceived as uncertain, and he may find it difficult to know how he should start with the task. At this stage, he needs support, for example, confirmation that he is on the right path. He wants to talk about what he intends to do and what might be difficult for him. When a few pieces fit into the "puzzle", he begins to see the structure of what he should learn or do. Once concerns are reduced, he can go ahead for himself and does not need to receive much support from his teacher. During the work process, he reworks his material several times to refine the results. If the work needs an introduction or a list of contents, it is something he does last of all. He needs to let the work emerge and does not see the structure from the beginning. It is something that shows itself during the work. Knowing the time frame helps him stay focused on the task and finish on time.

SUMMARY OF SIMON'S NEEDS IN HIS LEARNING PROCESS:

I would first like to hear. The teacher can tell his/her own story connected to what we should learn, after that I can start reading the text.

I want to talk with others about what we are going to do. If I do talk, my thoughts become clearer to me, and it will help me to get new ideas.

There should not be too much information at once. If that happens, I easily feel confused and find it difficult to know where to start.

It is good if there are not too many choices. Too many things to choose from takes me a long time to pick out the most essential.

It is very important that I have a good connection with my teacher and feel that he/she likes me.

I may need help in the start of a task because there are so many ways to go. Once I get started, I can continue working on my own.

During the process, I would like to show my teacher how I think I will do my task and get his/her feedback.

It is good if I have a time frame; otherwise it is easy that I take in too much time or have trouble keeping on track.

AMANDA – AN EMOTIONAL-MENTAL LEARNING PROCESS

When I want to learn something, it is good if the teacher first explains and gives me different options so that I can choose how I start with my task. I want to discuss, come up with new ideas, test new approaches, and adapt them to what we decided. I like to start working in a group, but would then like to work on my own. When I am almost finished, I can reconcile work with my teacher or group.

I often get the leadership role in the group, without knowing how it happens. I often become selected when my classmates make any choice of leadership. I do not mind it, because then I can keep track. No, I mean that then I can bring the work forward and know what happens. I think that I have more patience now than I had when I was younger, and I can listen more to others. Earlier I would have a difficult time completing a task, but now I have learned to complete it in a better way. Now I finish my work, not just a little here and a little there. I have a better ability to wait for my turn in a group. I wait and see what happens.

Even though Amanda, like Simon, is Emotionally centered, her process differs a lot from his. Both start with an auditory signal, but listen in a completely different way. She begins by listening to the teacher and trying to catch up on what she finds meaningful in what is told. Is there something new? Is there something that can be done in a new way? Several ideas immediately pop into her mind as she connects to what she hears. If the teacher is not too detailed in his/her descriptions, and Amanda discovers something new in what she hears, she is both enthusiastic and committed. She wants to get on with her job as quickly as possible. She needs to try and experiment. It is by starting to work that she can see the next step. The structure is there from the beginning, but it is flexible and can be changed. This is unlike Simon where the structure will show up further on in the process.

Amanda would like to start by talking to someone about her task, and then she wants to work by herself. During the work, she needs to reconnect with her group or her teacher. Then she needs to know that she is on track. If the teacher comes in too early in her work, she can become irritated. She wants to show the teacher when she deems it appropriate and will ask if she needs help. Another thing that is very important in the Emotional-mental learning process is to have the opportunity to influence the task, often by coming up with suggestions on how to go on with the task. If Amanda is told to do something without seeing the meaning of the task from her own viewpoint, she can lose engagement and energy. She might even refuse to do the task. She is responsive to her workgroup's needs and is often the one who talks for the group. The group strongly affects her, even though it may not always be noticeable.

A teacher self-identified to have the Physical-emotional process told me that she now found it easier to manage and respond to students with the Emotional-mental process. She had realized that they were not so "insensitive" or lacked empathy, for example, in conflict situations, something she previously thought. Now she knows that what she interpreted as insensitivity was more about the need to focus on how a conflict will be resolved. She is no longer primarily focused on how the persons involved in the conflict feel.

SUMMARY OF AMANDA'S NEEDS IN THE LEARNING PROCESS

I would first like to hear my teachers tell me; it may well be about something new and unknown.

I would like to discuss my and other people's ideas. I will have seeds of ideas, although I realize that not every idea can be implemented.

I do not need to have too much information from the teacher in the beginning of a job. It is more fun to have to discover it for myself and decide how I should complete the task.

I like to experiment and try new things.

When I need help, I will ask my teacher; he/she need not come and ask me how things are going while I work. I will ask for help when I need it. I want to decide when I will showcase my work. It may be when I think it is clear.

It is important that my teacher is fair. Injustice is the worst thing I know.

Physically centered learning processes

The Physical-emotional and Physical-mental processes differ significantly from those based on an Emotional centering. For teachers who have an Emotional centering, it may be difficult to understand those who have a Physical centering. To give you an insight into how people with Physical processes of learning, let's go back to Jenny with the Physical-emotional process and Malin with the Physical-mental.

JENNY – A PHYSICAL-EMOTIONAL LEARNING PROCESS

When I want to learn new things, I have to understand the context of the task, how the arrangement looks, how the task should be carried out, and what the expected outcome is. I cannot just start from a small part. Therefore, perhaps my teachers think I do not understand or am stupid. Often, I need to ask again because of my need to get all of the details of the task. I want to sit and think. I need time to myself before I start. In my head, I create a picture of how I should proceed. It may seem as if I just sit and do nothing before I start. But in my case, the teacher or group have not seen and understood everything going on in my mind when I think and collect all the facts.

Once I receive all of the information that I need, and the plan is ready, then I start working to read, write, or produce something. It can be quite extensive, because I want to have all of the details of the whole in what I create. I need time to finish my work at my own pace without getting stressed. I think that I have become much better at opting out what is not essential. I have also become better at and can say no when it is appropriate. Today I also say what I think about a matter even if I do not have the full picture.

Jenny's learning process starts as kinesthetic/tactile. She needs to see and experience with all senses what she is going to learn. To fulfill the need of the Physical-emotional student's learning, all of the materials related to the job should be available in the classroom.

It is most helpful if the materials are there days before the task instructions are given. There should be an opportunity to walk around and feel, see, hear, taste, and smell everything. Jenny experiences so much through her senses, observes everything around her, absorbs, takes in, and connects to a whole. It is an organic process where she collects detailed data and facts to understand. The collection goes hand-in-hand with the processing. Old knowledge is added to the new order to be used in the future.

It is important that she feels peace and harmony in the classroom during the work. She may need to withdraw from the group to think through the task. As she often does not say anything until she has the whole picture, it is important that we wait and hear out her answers and comments. When she learns new things, it may take some time before everything is in place. With old and familiar things, however, she performs quickly.

When she incorporates the new knowledge to herself, she does it without selecting. She does not consider it necessary to sort initially; eventually she sorts out what is most useful. While she collects the relevant facts, she may ignore the teacher's emotional and verbal abundance. Once the structure begins to become visible for her, Jenny can build the wholeness that is so important for her. Students with this learning process often have been misjudged in schools. Perhaps it is because most teachers have an Emotional centering, and their teaching is based on their own way of learning and knowing. They do not understand these students' way of learning.

One mother told me that her daughter, as she understood, had the Physical-emotional process. The daughter participated in the school's swimming classes in the second grade. The teacher had told the mother that the girl sat on the side of the swimming pool and watched her classmates practicing swimming. The swimming instructor tried every way to get her down in the water, but she refused. Then the day came when everyone would compete to swim for the "fish", the first swimming badge. The mother felt a little worried and decided to sit in the swimming hall cafeteria where she could see into the pool, but not be visible herself. "I could not believe it" she exclaimed. "My daughter went down into the water and swam the 25 meters. I do not know how she had learned, but she could swim."

When a student sits quietly and does not immediately respond to a question, it may be that the information was too sketchy. It is very important to give space and time, so that these students will be able to think calmly and be able to speak their minds and come up with their answer.

Because students need to see the practical linked to the theoretical, there should be laboratory teaching materials in as many disciplines as possible. A natural situation for Physical-emotional students is to let them observe, and in peace and quiet, be in the situation, to assimilate the information. It seems as if they are taking in visually and quietly processing the information. Once they decide what they should learn, then they are able to proceed with the task.

SUMMARY OF JENNY'S NEEDS IN THE LEARNING PROCESS:

I need to see, hear, and do to be able to learn in the best way for me.

I begin by taking in everything that my teacher and classmates say. It may be too much information, and at first, I do not know how to handle it.

I usually think that everything I hear and read is equally important. I need help to remove what is not so important in a task. I may also need help to structure it.

I think I need time. It can take a long time to learn new things, but when I learn something I have it forever. I think I have a good memory.

I do not want to throw myself into something that I do not know much about; I'd rather wait until I have more information.

I think the details are important, such as when someone tells me about his/her dog. Then I want to know the breed, age, color, if it is smooth-haired or curly, the kennel the dog came from, and what it likes to eat, etc.

I feel stressed if I do not get finished with my task at my own pace. If the teacher targets me, I become blocked and do not know what I should do. Then I just sit and watch and understand nothing.

It is good if I get to know how much time we have for the task. I then feel calmer and can prepare my work in a good way.

MALIN – A PHYSICAL-MENTAL LEARNING PROCESS

When I need to learn new things and the purpose is not clear to me, I find it difficult to begin the task. I just sit and think about what it means, wondering about the time frame. I wonder why I am doing this, and what is the expected outcome? If I do not have this clear to me, I have little interest in doing the task. However, if I have been told the purpose, goals, and time frame, I start by trying to see the goal and what this will lead to. Then I lay out a plan for the work and work methodically towards the goal. Maybe my teacher thinks that I am hard to deal with sometimes. Since I so consciously go about working my way towards the goal that I set up, I am not inclined to change my plans or opinions. When something happens to affect my plan, or if a decision is changed, I sometimes react strongly to it. I would rather not change a decision if I do not see that it leads to something better. Today I find it easier to be flexible and can have alternative plans in what I have to do. I have more flexibility.

When Malin is going to do something it begins with a question: What should I do? For whom do I do it? To what use? What is the expected outcome, and what are the time frames? When she receives the aim and objectives in a clear manner, she can start. She

43

examines the factual knowledge she has of the subject and acquires new knowledge that she considers necessary. This is a process that may take more or less time, depending on previous knowledge and how interested she is in the task. If there is something that she thinks is interesting and important to learn, she wants to know everything and gather as much factual information about the subject as possible. She says in her earlier story: "When something is interesting, then I can dig all the way to China." However, if there is something that is not so interesting, she can cope with fewer facts and relatively quickly get the task done. By creating new models or refining and reworking old, she can better understand how things work. One example is with her language lesson. When she begins to get an overview and summarize the contents, she emphasizes the new words and new meanings. The words and sentences are then written into a special book. The new becomes her focus, not what she already knows. Maps, charts, and graphs can be very helpful in her learning process. If a theme is planned for work in class, it is very helpful for Malin to get the actual information as a summary of the task's content. Then she can participate more actively in the discussions in her class. As Malin's knowledge is based on facts, it can be difficult to spontaneously fantasize about something that has no basis in reality.

Magnus, one of my former students, became upset because I changed one thing one day. We had planned for an outdoors lesson, and I had said to the students the day before. "Tomorrow we will meet at the big tree in the schoolyard. There is no need to go into the school before we leave." When I arrived at the school the next day, all of the students except Magnus were standing on the stairs of the school. The only one who stood by the tree was Magnus. I did not think much of it, but called him to come to the rest of us to receive instructions for the day. He got upset and said: "You said we would meet at the tree, and that's where I want to wait."

To change a decision can be hard; you have to convince the student that the change is a better idea.

Summary of Malin's needs in her learning process:

I learn by reading, seeing, and doing. It can be useful if there are pictures or diagrams, maps, and key words. Then I learn more easily.

I always want to have the purpose clear to me. If I do not have a purpose stated, then I must try to create the purpose myself. Then it can take much longer to start the task.

When the purpose is clear, I can start my work. I start to think how it will look when it is finished. Then I go back and begin to gradually work my way towards the goal.

I want to learn everything in a subject that I am interested in. Then it is important that all detail is included.

I want facts that I can relate to reality. Just imagining can be hard for me. Therefore, it is not so easy when my teacher wants me to use my imagination in essays for example.

It is important to use the right words and be credible. If anyone just says things straight out that they do not have the evidence for, I find it difficult to listen.

It may be hard to change me when I am committed to something. There must be a strong reason to change something that works well. If something is to change, then I must see the advantages of it clearly.

Mentally centered learning process

Students with Mental centering may be relatively rare in our classes and in our workplaces. In their investigations, Seagal and Horne (1997, 2004) note that people with this centering are few. The rarity causes one to interpret their way in a negative manner. It may be that one says: "He has no social skills." "He does not seem to care." "Why do I get no response from her?" Think how wrong it is when we only use ourselves as the measure and not try to understand other ways of being.

It makes me think of a lesson when I introduced a work about Springtime for grade 2. I started the lesson by playing "Spring" by Edward Grieg, and then, in my opinion, after the music I made a valid and good description of the task. I was pleased with my introduction, and after a while I remember telling the students; "Now you can go ahead and start to work with your task." Annelie, my little Mental-physical student approached me and said, "Ms. Berit, what is it exactly that you mean for us to do? I do not understand?" She looked serious and a little challenging at me. Why did she not understand my instruction? Upon my own reflection, I realized what I had done. I had presented the task in a natural way for me, many words, associative and emotive, and not at all through Annelie's need for facts and structure.

GUSTAV – A MENTAL-PHYSICAL LEARNING PROCESS

When I want to learn things, it is good if I'm going to learn what I think is important. But really, all things in school are important. So, it is just to learn. Sometimes it takes a long time for me to be done with my details, perhaps because I am very careful in almost everything I do. I can get very frustrated if I do not understand a task from beginning to end. Regarding the use of the right words in the right context, it probably is nothing I usually think of. But I think it is important that the teacher expresses himself/herself clearly and precisely. I write down as much as possible of what the teacher says. It helps me keep focused when I am listening. When I write things down, I select what is most essential. Sometimes I write only important key words. I have no problem with listening if it does not become too much or go on too long.

I think that I now have more understanding of the value of being in a group, the feeling of being part of a group. I feel safer if I have the facts about something I have to change. There is much to be done based on facts. If a moment of change comes in the end of the task, it is difficult for me. If it is necessary, I want it to come early in the process. Perhaps it has to do with how many times I have to think through several aspects before making a decision. I think I have more to learn about being flexible.

Gustav begins by gaining an overview of the whole task, where it starts and where it is expected to finish. He asks how important it is and how much time he will use. When he has gotten the target clear, and the overall structure, he begins the task to lay out its "rails" to the target. The structure is there, without him thinking about it. Based on the main characteristics of the task, he adds the details he considers necessary for the task to be solved in a good way. He is logical and structured, methodically, and step-by-step he solves the task.

As the teacher, it is important to think about connecting with the Mental-physical student in a personal way. Because they do not emphasize themselves, they do not talk about their own ideas and thoughts. Therefore, you have to ask questions and provide space for them to come up with their answers and comments. Because the student is accurate and precise, and wants precise instructions, we should not be multi-focused or use a fuzzy language.

SUMMARY OF GUSTAV'S NEEDS IN THE LEARNING PROCESS:

I need to get an overall perspective on what I am expected to learn. I remember when we had lessons about Sweden, it would have been good if we had started with an outline of Sweden and then picked out the different provinces, but we did exactly the opposite. We began to study each landscape. I got bored after a few landscapes, because I did not see the whole picture.

I prefer to get an overview by reading, and then I listen to what the teacher says.

I do not want to answer the obvious questions. I do not like to talk just for talking's sake.

I prefer individual work, but also have learned to like working in a group. The group should not be too large. I can start working for myself and later present my material in the group. The teacher should not talk too much or fan out in different directions. It is best to stick to the point and be clear and precise.

I need time to process my material until I am satisfied with it. If I do not get time to do so, I become frustrated.

I do not go in and interrupt a conversation, especially if the group is large or there are people I do not know well.

SUMMARY – CHARACTERISTICS AND NEEDS IN THE LEARNING PROCESS.

Emotional-physical

- Want to start auditory, to hear about the task, and to have a dialogue.
- Process thoughts, ideas, and feelings in conversation with oneself and others.
- Relate new knowledge to personal experiences.
- Sensitive to other people's tone of voice and the way in which knowledge is conveyed.
- Need to have good relationships with people in the environment, mainly the teacher.
- It is important to have good relations in the group for joint learning.
- Can easily lose focus if too many pieces are inserted, or if the material is too unstructured.

Emotional-mental

- Want to start auditory, to hear about the task, and to have a dialogue about what should be done.

- Get new knowledge in spontaneous discussions with others.
- Want to quickly start a task; it leads to ensuring continued attachment to the work.
- Relate to ideas, one's own and others.
- Are not particularly interested in the details, select those deemed necessary.
- Appreciate the challenges, want to experiment and try new ideas.
- Problem-solving stimulates learning.
- Can easily create a structure of the work at the beginning, which can be changed and modified during the work without issue.

Physical-emotional

- Want to start in a tactile/kinesthetic way. Experience with all senses and be in the learning environment.
- Good if the theory and practice can be mixed.
- Start to collect all information without selecting, sorting, or structure. In terms of new knowledge, it is a process that can take time.
- The structure comes later in the process.
- Generally have a very good memory.
- Link to the context and the whole connecting to prior knowledge to understand the new.
- Important to complete a task in an accurate, detailed, and precise manner.

Physical-mental

- Want to start by trying to understand the purpose and the practical benefits of a task.
- Bring up facts/data related to the purpose and objectives.

- Link to the big picture and work strategically and methodically.
- Are both system builders and systematic.
- Connect background facts to present facts for future knowledge.
- Importance of pre-understanding for the accomplishment of a task.
- Charts, diagrams, tables, and models are key.
- Need own time to synchronize the task, the body, and the surroundings in different rhythms.

Mental-physical

- Want to start visually, to see and read, then start to work alone and after that, there may be a need to discuss with others about the task.
- Structured, logical, focused, and selective in collecting facts.
- Accurate and precise in their work.
- Have view/perspective, can easily go from macro to micro level and back again.
- Willing to revise and refine the task a number of times, making it as precise as possible.
- Prefer to work alone or in a small group.
- Express themselves objectively and are fact-oriented, rather than personally relating.

From TO LEARN IN DIFFERENT WAYS (Seagal, Horne and Bergström, 1999)

COMMUNICATION

Do we have time to stop and really listen to each other? Or do we get so strained by all of the impressions and diversity of sounds that we turn off our real listening? Do we give ourselves the time to understand what another person is saying?

Perhaps we already have begun to create something out from our perception of what is being said, even before the conversation is really started. Listening to one another is an art, something you have to practice and learn for yourself. It is much more than just hearing the words and responding to them. When we truly listen to each other "I listen to you because I feel respect for you and what you have to say. I want to get to know you. I want to understand you better."

Some of us speak and listen at the same time. Others need to quit and think after listening, and then are able to speak. Some use many words to answer a question and can blossom in vivid descriptions. Others are more laconic and only want to convey what is clearly and safely anchored. In conversation, we believe we know what the other person says and that he/she has the same understanding of the words that we ourselves use. That is not always the case. A word or a certain phrase can be perceived quite differently by various people. We should be careful to listen and find out if what we perceive is what the other person intended. One example is the word **overview**. A person who has a Mental centering may mean what one sees from a distance, structured, and only the main points. Someone who has a Physical centering might interpret the word as a place where one has all of the details in place and can see the big picture in all its complexity. The overview for an Emotionally centered person might include the perceived moods of others in the room.

Once I had a seminar with a group of people in the department of human resources of a company. Since I only had a few hours for my presentation, I decided to talk about our different communication needs. It became very clear for the participants how differently we interpret words.

I encouraged the participants to think about something that was important to them in communication with others. After a while, the participants wrote down their needs on a whiteboard. Two women with very different personalities had both written that honest communication was the most important thing. When I asked one woman what she meant by an honest communication, she replied: "It is when you directly say what you think and feel without a lot of words around it. I do not like it when people beat around the bush, and use euphemisms in place of what they have to say." The other woman then said: "No, that is not what I mean by an honest communication. That is when I know that the person that I am speaking with does not have a hidden agenda, nor do I. It means that they don't say one thing yet mean another. Then I feel it at once, even if I cannot pinpoint what it is, and I cannot listen fully to what is being said. I feel insecure as I am considering just what the person means by their words.

It is not just the words we use to communicate. Body language is very important in communication. Some of us use the body and facial expressions more than others to emphasize the verbal communication. Eye contact is also very important, and often that is manifested clearly in people who are Emotionally centered. Even in many very young children, we can see a lively body language and the need for eye contact. Others have a more limited body language, and eyes are not so focused on the person they are in contact with.

Facial expression and body language are closely linked to the culture we live in. In a more emotional culture, the body language becomes livelier, regardless of peoples' different basic processes, whereas in another culture body language may be more limited. On one occasion, I had a seminar in Israel and lived in that country for a number of weeks. When I returned to Sweden, I realized I had taken it upon myself to resume the Swedish "suit" of more limited and less expressive body language.

The rhythm of the communication is also part of how we express ourselves. In people who are Emotionally centered, communication can billow out like a waltz, in a giving and taking. Others may complete a sentence that you started, and this is not considered impolite or an interruption. For people with a Mental or Physical centering, conversation is more steady, thoughtful, structured, and with clear boundaries.

To understand the communication needs of people with different processes, we can listen to the phrases and words that are used most frequently. Some words can be especially important for people with a certain process. One often hears Emotional-physical people use the word "feel". "How does it feel?" "How do you feel about this?" "This does not feel good to me" and so on.

If our experience is that we cannot reach a person, it may be because the person has a different communication process than our own. When we are aware of the differences, we can try to adapt to the other person's needs. It is important to try to listen to the central themes based on the person's way of expressing himself/herself. Timing is also important. We have different needs of time when it comes to talk. It is important to appreciate and understand that one way is not better than the other. The central themes in communication are how words are pronounced, the rhythm or timing, and the person's relation to time. How it is said is also something to listen for.

VARIOUS ASPECTS OF COMMUNICATION

Emotional-physical communication process

CENTRAL THEMES: emotion, togetherness, relationships, processing, harmony, sharing.

TIME: one has a personal relationship to the past and to the present.

LISTEN FOR: feelings, personal interpretations, variations in feelings, and a multicultural focus.

Simon says this about his communication needs:

"It must be a sensitivity for feelings and experiences. It happens often when someone tells me something that I remember an incident similar to what I hear. And I will tell the person my experience, not in any way to interrupt, but rather to emphasize what I hear told. I can very easily pick up different moods and feelings of others and connect to them. I can do that even if nothing is said. When I feel insecure with someone, I will be quiet and pull back. When everything feels good, I think I can be good at conversation as I so easily can put myself into another person's situation."

Associative thinking is going on all the time when interacting with others, but also as an internal communication. Words and mind go hand-in-hand. There is a need to shape the thoughts. It may be useful for persons who do not have the Emotional-physical process to know that what is said are not completed thoughts. It just can be part of the thinking. You can simply ask the question: "Are you sure about that? Are your thoughts clear?" It would clarify many misunderstandings when the person's thoughts are taken as a firm decision or position on an issue, when in fact their expression is part of an ongoing process.

A lot of what is said depends on what happens in the environment and the current situation. We must allow time for the verbal process, because it is through it that the Emotional-physical person's thoughts are clarified. Simon says that he has a sensitivity for his feelings and their relationship to his own experiences, and that it is natural to connect them. In communication, he picks up other people's feelings easily, and to become absorbed in a dialogue it must feel genuine. If there seems to be a hidden agenda, that will create anxiety and uncertainty.

To reach a person who has the Emotional-physical process, we can ask questions like: "How do you feel about this?" "Does this have a personal meaning for you?" "What is most important in what we are going to do?" "Do you need more time to process this for yourself?" "Or do you prefer to talk about it?" "If I understand you correctly, is this what you meant?"

Emotional-mental communication process

CENTRAL THEMES: justice, respect, innovation, ideas, responsibilities, a forward direction in the communication.

TIME: has a forward planning into the near future, sometimes linked to past events.

LISTEN FOR: Forward movement, ideas, flexibility.

Amanda thinks she is direct and targeted in her communication. She would like to begin a talk with a broad picture and with few details. Quickly she forms an opinion of what you are talking about. Too many details make her lose interest. It is best when the communication is like a tennis match, the ball goes over the net, back and forth quickly from one to the other.

"If I do not get answers on an idea or question that I am given, I think that everyone likes the idea. If nobody says anything, I go on with it. I can be

very surprised if I then hear that I just went on, not listening to others. Sometimes others feel run over. It was not my intention. If someone gets too verbose and blossoms into too many associations, I have trouble listening. Then I start easily thinking of other unrelated things." Amanda says that a friend of hers who also has the Emotional-mental process said: *"Sometimes I think I have two mouths and one ear." It can be hard to listen when someone is talking too much. I am too eager to get to the point."*

To meet the communication needs of people with this process, we must remember not to be too detailed when the conversation starts. We have to give the image of the whole picture; the details can come later when we catch people's attention and interest.

When Amanda feels stressed in her communication, she can become very direct. Then it is good to know that what is said is not meant as personal criticism. It is more a question of finding the way forward, for example, the solution to a problem. The focus is on what will be done, not the person who said it.

It is good to open the communication with questions about the ideas that the person may have: "Do you have any idea on how we should start with this? What key focus should we have? What do you want to take responsibility for? How much time do you think that it will take?"

Between the two Emotionally centered groups misunderstandings and conflicts in communication rarely occur. People with this centering start in the Emotional principle and then take different approaches depending on whether you have the Emotional-physical process or Emotional-mental process. The following story is an example of how things can turn out.

A Wednesday morning began when a colleague and I, both Emotionally centered, were discussing a newspaper article about giving grades in the lower school. We had totally opposite views, and the discussion was both inappropriate and too personal. At the end of the day, when all lessons were finished and the students had gone home, we sat down to go over what had happened between us. We sorted out the concepts and went away to our homes as friends. Yet something felt wrong, and I could not stop thinking of how it had happened. When I went home I told my husband about the conflict and my experience of it. The last thing I did before I fell asleep was to once again go through what had happened. Two days later, when I met my colleague, I brought up the subject and said: "Look, we need to talk more about what happened last Wednesday; it does not feel good to me." She looked at me with surprise and said: "What was it that happened on Wednesday?" In reacting to this, it was easy for negative thoughts to turn up in me, and it would have damaged our relationship if I had said: "Yes, what happened probably was not as important to you as for me, so insensitive as you are!"

Instead, I could now think in a different way and say: "But this was what happened last Wednesday and I need to talk more about it." When she heard me repeat what had happened, she remembered the incident that she had already left behind, and could return to me in the conversation.

Physical-emotional communication process

CENTRAL THEMES: context, practical, details, time, wholeness, accurate, experience.

TIME: both personal and universal, from past to present and into the future.

LISTEN FOR: FACTS, continuity, context, details, descriptions, stories.

Jenny says:

"In communication, it is important to get enough information to be able to see the context and the entirety of what is said. I can get very frustrated if someone wants a quick answer when I do not have what I need. Then I become quiet and perhaps answer: 'I do not know'. But it is not that I do

not know, I just have not had time to think. Sometimes I ask many questions, about things that others have not thought of or might not think are particularly important. I think people often misjudge me; perhaps they think I do not have an opinion on what is said, but of course I do. I just need some time to think, because I do not want to blurt out an answer or opinion. It is also important that I get to speak to the point. It is important that there is trustworthiness in what is being said. It is better to wait to say something until you really know what it is that you want to say and have a proper response to a question. To get an overall perspective, necessary details must be given to be able to see the entire context. Then I can come up with my view."

How do we meet a person with the Physical-emotional process so that our communication will be as good as possible? The first thing we need to consider is to speak calmly, not to rush off with words and thoughts in every possible direction. Because this person is listening to everything you say and all the time trying to get a full picture of what the talk is about, it can be confusing if you are too fast and using too many words. Questions that might be good to ask: "What facts do you want to have? How much time do you think you will need? What could have happened earlier that affects what we are doing now? You may need time to think this through. Do you need more information?" We must know that even if some of us experience the communication process between us as a bit tedious, often the result of what is communicated will be correct and complete.

Physical-mental communication process

CENTRAL THEMES: aim, background, credibility, strategic context, plan, practical, models, and designs.

TIME: relevant time/now, the elapsed time with the direction into the future.

LISTEN FOR: intention, purpose, relevant background information, strategies to achieve the purpose.

This is what Malin says about her communication:

"For me, communication needs to be factual and objective. I want to have a structure in the exchange of ideas. I also need to know the purpose of our communication. I'll get a quick overview, what it is about, and then I can decide at what level I am going to participate. If I am interested in, and have knowledge of what you are talking about, I can be quite talkative. And I will tell you everything I know of the subject. When that happens, I can see that others do not really listen to everything I have to say. It seems like they turn off, and it can feel a little hurtful. It can be annoying with too many personal feelings and opinions in a communication. Too much talk makes me confused. I think I am good at listening and creating a security for others in the conversation, and I want to help solve the problem."

People with this process want the communication to be precise, clear and logical. Since their thinking is an internal process, they can be quiet a long time before a response is given to a question or statement. Language rhythm is smooth, and they prefer to talk one at a time.

If something is not clear, questions are asked to ascertain. Questions that we can ask a person who has the Physical-mental process can be: "Have you got a clear purpose to the task? Do you need to know more? How much time do you think that you will need? Is there anything else we need to take into consideration before we begin?"

For those who are Emotionally centered, it may be difficult to understand the Physical-mental person's communication needs. One should not express their own feelings and opinions without having evidence of what is said. A person with the Emotional-physical basic process, where speech and thought go hand-in-hand, can be both irritating and disturbing to someone with the Physical-mental process.

Mental-physical communication process

CENTRAL THEMES: values, view/perspective, clarity, structure, purpose, vision, precision.

TIME: long-term, the future

LISTEN FOR: the essence, structures, values, objectivity, and detachment

For Gustav, communications must be clear and complete. For him it can be difficult to follow a conversation that contains too many personal opinions and emotions being played out. He says:

"If there are too many words and too many feelings, I have difficulty following a conversation in all directions. I would like to finish what I have to say and not be interrupted before I finish talking. Quite often what happens is that others go into the conversation before I'm finished, and when that happens, I will become quiet. I am not the person who enters and interrupts a conversation. I think that everyone should speak to the point. I do not share with any one my inner thoughts and feelings, those I save for the few people who I know deeply."

Gustav becomes frustrated when communication is too multi-focused and emotional. Then he loses the exact meaning of the words. A boy with the Mental-physical process came home from school and was upset that he did not understand what the teacher meant when she gave homework for the next day. When his mother asked what the teacher had told the students about the homework, the boy replied: "She just stood there and said blah, blah, blah, blah. I could not hear the words because it was so much talk." The child turns off when he/she does not understand what is being said. When we notice it, it is very important to try to ask the relevant questions: "Have I been clear enough in what I say? What questions do you have about what was said? What do you think? Is this interesting for you?" We must allow Gustav to get into the conversation and not interrupt him when he is talking.

People who are Emotionally-centered experience communication with a person who has the Mental-physical process in the same way as when they communicate with a person with the Physical-mental process. Similarities exist but also many differences. With both there may not be a spontaneous response, and the person does not show as clear a body language. Then it is easy to be misjudged. Perhaps we believe that he/she is not engaged or listening. We can also interpret it as rejection which is not what it is about. It is important to be observant of the more subtle signals to meet the needs of the person.

As I said earlier, *there is no value difference between the processes*. No one way is preferred over the others. We all have a role to play. The conversation has a better outcome when we recognize and respect the differences in conversational needs and styles, for example, when we come with different ideas for how to solve a problem. Sometimes there is a need for objectivity, sometimes creative and innovative thinking, and sometimes practical approaches. When we unconditionally listen to what everyone has to contribute and make use of various abilities, we discover the pluralism that exists and how enriching true communication can be.

Ragnhild N. Grodal (1990), in her book entitled *Forandring Fryder? ("Change is Joy?")*, described our differences in a communication perspective. It is translated here:

It is important for us to find balance in everything that we see, feel, and do. Something that for me has become very important is that I understand that some of us have a more objective, factual style. Others seem to have a more subjective, personal style. It may be necessary to distinguish between the different communication cultures to better understand the differences and to avoid misunderstanding.

SUMMARY OF THE DIFFERENT COMMUNICATION NEEDS:

Emotional-physical

- It is important to have a personal connection in the conversation.
- What comes up and what is said depends often on the situation when the conversation takes place.
- There must be sensitivity to emotions and relationships and to one's own and other's experiences.
- One has a sensitivity to and easily picks up other people's moods and feelings. Therefore, dialogue must be genuine; there must be no hidden agenda. Listens first to who you are and then what you say.

Emotional-mental

- Straight and targeted in the communication. Asks direct questions about what is unclear.
- Communications are forward thinking; often in dialogue with others.
- Want the overall picture. Too many details can make it so that they lose interest in the communication.
- Listens to what you say, not primarily who you are.

Physical-emotional

- Early in the communication wants a picture of the context and the whole.
- Facts and many details, and time for reflection are important in communication.
- Listens to all that is said to create as complete and clear a picture as possible before responding.

Physical-mental

- Wants the communication objective and clear.

- Important to know the purpose and get a quick overview.

- Context and overall are important but not too many personal experiences and feelings in the conversation.

- The communication must be focused on a problem-solving function.

Mental-physical

- The communication must be clear, precise, and logical.

- As the thinking is an internal process, there is often a moment of silence in the conversation while thinking about how to respond.

- Language rhythm is smooth, gives space for everyone to talk without interruption.

- It is important that the words are precise so that no misunderstanding occurs.

- Communication is often factual and objective, not personal.

PERSONAL DEVELOPMENT

ALL OF US HAVE A GIFT FOR GROWING

All cultures and societies create their own patterns, norms, and values. From the day that we are born, we are affected by them. We adapt and become part of that culture. For some of us, it is easy, for others, more difficult. If we easily behave based on what we think is right and blend into a context that is the norm, we are rewarded by society. It is something that starts very early. Already in primary school you see the children that easily adapt to the demands of society. They are the social children, those we believe will "succeed". We also meet children we regard as a bit odd, that might not so easily crack the social code, children we find fault with and we have problems with. Children who cannot make themselves accepted in the same way as the "successful."

With the new understanding of diversity you now have, you do not need to assess people based on social norms and values. You can see and understand different people's qualities and abilities. Instead of narrowly assessing what is different from yourself, you can, with curiosity and joy, value and accept diversity.

In order to develop, the starting point are our three parts again, Mental, Emotional and Physical – the three universal principles which are indeed the building blocks. The goal of personal development is to have a balanced interaction among them as each will support us in different ways. We can consciously choose to highlight the principle that we think needs to be strengthened and developed. Yet in order to more deeply understand ourselves, we must be aware of both the quantitative distribution and the qualitative development of the three principles. I will illustrate what this could mean by two girls, Linda and Johanna. They attended the same class in 9th grade, and when I first met them, I could not at first believe that they had the same process, the Emotional-physical, because they were so different.

Each girl's process of communication and learning starts in the Emotional principle, their centering. This is their way of relating in a flexible and associative way. With both girls, there is a direct link between the centering and the Physical principle. This means that they radiate out from their feelings to meet people and the environment. This interest in sensory input, context and diversity creates opportunities to communicate, learn, and solve problems.

Linda does not show her feelings so easily, even though they constantly affect her very much. She often is calm and quiet in large groups, and many perceive her as shy and insecure. She is not the one who initiates a conversation with someone she does not know well. Once she feels safe and accepted, she can be spontaneous, express feelings, and be talkative.

Johanna, in contrast, is like a storm that takes in a lot, is fast, and spontaneous. She often speaks without thinking. When something goes slightly wrong, she can easily change her mind. She is expressive when it comes to feelings, and she often meets others in her surroundings with many hugs, laughter, or even crying. She talks a lot and has a lively body language.

How can it be that they can be so different and yet have the same process? We can all, regardless of our process, be more or less extroverted. We are using the example of Linda and Johanna to take a deeper look at how the quantitative distribution of the three principles can affect the expression of basic processes so differently. If you think of the three principles taking up space in ones being, then the centering principle can be seen as taking the largest space, the second principle less space, and the third principle the least. Because this is a schematic way of describing a phenomenon, it is important that we see it as such, and regard it as an understanding of the dynamic interaction among the three principles – not as a static description of how a person is.

Can it be that Linda's Emotional principle, in a quantitative way, does not take up so much space and therefore is not as visible to others? From the outside, it looks as if the Physical principle has a larger space, the principle that often makes one more quiet, more thoughtful, and more group-oriented.

In Johanna, the Emotional principle is more visible; it helps her to be more spontaneous and have more association ability. Possibly her Emotional principle takes up more space than Linda's.

The quantitative distribution of principles can be seen in all of us when we are children and seems to be almost unchanged through life. However, what happens during the lifetime is that the principles can change qualitatively. When all three principles are developed, we get a better balance, and the result is visible in that we become more mature. We speak of this as *integration*. According to Seagal and Horne (1997), the third principle is the key to continued personal development. An integrated personality has the ability to express all three principles in a balanced way.

For the two girls in this example who are both Emotional-physical, it is their third principle, the Mental principle, that can help them get a qualitatively better balance between the principles. By consciously activating the Mental principle, Linda may gain greater stability, selectivity, and confidence. For Johanna's part, the interaction with the third or Mental principle creates a sense of calm and stability that allows her to manage her feelings with greater objectivity and caution.

To develop an integrated personality means to nourish and integrate the Mental, Emotional and Physical principles in everyday forms of expression, such as a clear, objective way of thinking (Mental), being kind-hearted and having good relationships with other people (Emotional), and the ability to become practical, systematic and effective (Physical).

The third principle

Awareness of our own third principle and its qualities makes it easier to see and understand our opportunities for development. It helps us to understand where we now find ourselves in our own personal development. As we have seen in the example above with the girls, even though we have the same basic process, we can express it quite differently depending on the quantitative distribution (which appears to be persistent throughout life) and the qualitative development (which can be deepened through life).

As previously mentioned, the centering principle of a person is the start of the various processes and demonstrates how we process information. Emotionally centered people process information in a non-linear, divergent, and associative way in relation to their environment. Physically centered people experience the world in a pragmatic way. Their centering means that they process the information in a systemic manner that involves a wholeness in relation all elements. Anyone who is Mentally centered processes the selected information in an objective and logical way with a detached perspective.

When we talk about process, we mean the close link between the centered principle and one of the other principles. It is the basic process that determines how we function and act in different situations, e.g. when we communicate with others or when we learn something new. The third principle helps us to achieve *balance* and, as mentioned, is a key for the development of all three principles. It is needed to *integrate*, to round out, and become whole.

To test how well our three principles are in *balance* or *integrated*, you can ask questions to your "third" principle.

For example:

QUESTIONS TO MY EMOTIONAL PRINCIPLE:

Am I in contact with my feelings?

Do I take into account other people's feelings, and can I create personal relationships with others?

Am I flexible when needed and can I use my creative ability?

QUESTIONS TO MY PHYSICAL PRINCIPLE:

Can I come up with practical and feasible suggestions about what should be done?

Can I have the patience, wait, and value the group?

Can I complete a task, the one for myself and others in a satisfactory manner?

QUESTION TO MY MENTAL PRINCIPLE:

Are my thoughts clear?

Can I be objective and logical?

Can I select and pick out what is most essential, for example, in a text? Can I have a long-term perspective?

Can I be visionary?

By consciously engaging all three principles, Emotional, Physical, and Mental, we can contribute to our well-being. We live in a time where speed is regarded as a virtue and where flexibility is a necessity for us to cope with our tasks. Keeping high tempo and being competitive means that sometimes we become highly stressed. We cannot always control our own environment or external circumstances; however, we can train ourselves to take a relaxed and peaceful approach. It is something that indeed helps us deal with life. Meditation and exercises of relaxation, focusing, and breathing are usually highly effective.

In order to take better advantage of our day, to see and understand our own conditions, and train ourselves to be more in the present, meditation and relaxation exercises are a good start to the day.

There are many different ways to do relaxation exercises. On the Internet, in bookstores, or in pharmacies, you can find CDs with both instructions and music. But keep in mind that it is important that you engage in exercises that allow you to "drain" the Mental, Emotional, and Physical part of you. Thus, no thoughts, emotions, or physical activity should be included in the exercise.

DEVELOPMENTAL PATH AND EXERCISES

The developmental path is like an upward spiral where, depending on the circumstances, energy moves the spiral in different planes. Sometimes we feel everything is easy, new knowledge is easily taken in, and energy flows in the body. The Emotional, Physical and Mental principles keep a dynamic and balanced interaction within us. Other times we feel the resistance and have difficulty both to think, to feel, and to act. It is as if the parts are pulling in different directions. The imbalance seems to cause us to fall back down to a lower level in the spiral. Then we have to consider the interaction between principles again. It is pretty easy to figure out which part must be strengthened in order to regain balance.

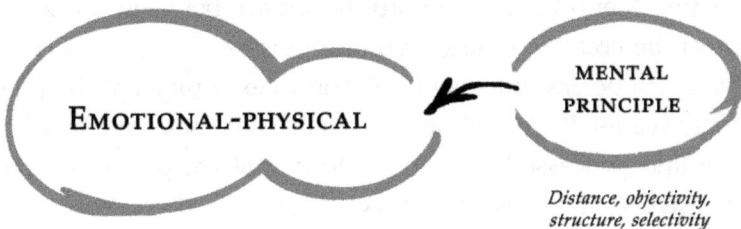

EMOTIONAL-PHYSICAL

MENTAL PRINCIPLE

Distance, objectivity, structure, selectivity

The Achilles heel for people with the Emotional-physical process can be their vulnerability to becoming a victim of circumstances. Personal desires and needs go unnoticed because of the feelings that you have to oblige and let others decide. It could be the parents, the teacher, or the manager's desire to get control of your life. With a more integrated Mental principle, you can easily create a boundary between yourself and others, to no longer be a part of other people's feelings and problems. It is easier to say no without feeling bad or guilty. With a greater ability to be selective, you are able to select activities and need not be involved in everything. You can concentrate on your own choices with greater objectivity and distance. When the three elements interact well, you can make your own choices with greater objectivity and distance when needed.

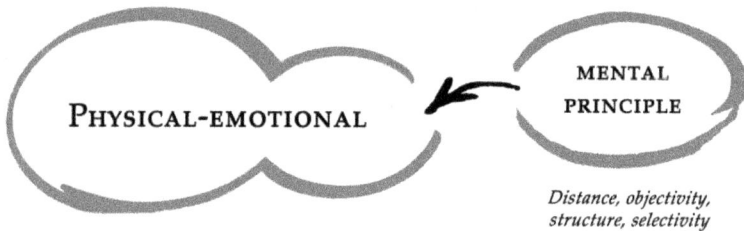

PHYSICAL-EMOTIONAL   MENTAL PRINCIPLE

Distance, objectivity, structure, selectivity

As a small child, or when one has not gone so far along the developmental path, the person with a Physical-emotional process feels part of a collective. We are all one. He/she is not able to set clear limits and listen to his/her "personal voice" or "true self". By that I mean, the child is not able to take a stand and say what he/she thinks. It can lead to becoming totally passive and blocked or stuck. With a more active Mental part, a helpful boundary between oneself and others can be created. One's own opinions can be expressed more clearly. It will be easier to say "no" and to express what the person genuinely wants. It also allows one to be more selective in what is taken in and processed. It is faster to be able to pick out what is essential when faced with a task. When the three components interact in a good way, this results in an awareness of one's own subjective self and a greater ability to have structure, perspective and selectivity. One becomes a person who calmly and methodically can demonstrate viable solutions, for example, to a problem.

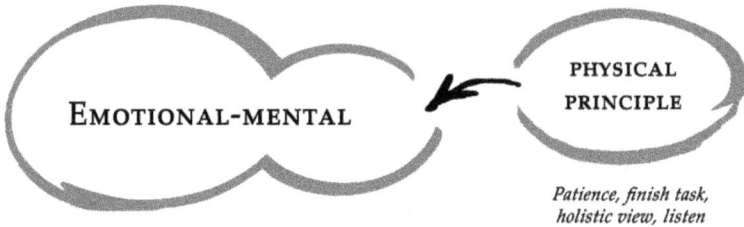

EMOTIONAL-MENTAL → PHYSICAL PRINCIPLE

Patience, finish task, holistic view, listen

For people with the Emotional-mental process, the Physical principle is the third. Without its inclusion, a person becomes controlling, taking power for him/herself and cannot see the needs of others. An example of this might be, if a decision is not taken quickly enough in the working group, the person can be insistent and just want to push through his/her own ideas and does not have the ability to listen or give time to others to come up with their proposals. As a small child, you become the "king in your own kingdom" and want to rule the world. When all three principles interact, you widen the scope to include others; you gain a greater ability to listen and to be patient, are able to wait and see details and their value. What happened yesterday can be important in what you are doing today. When the Physical principle is integrated, it leads to a greater awareness of one's own actions. You own the ideas and thoughts of the entire group.

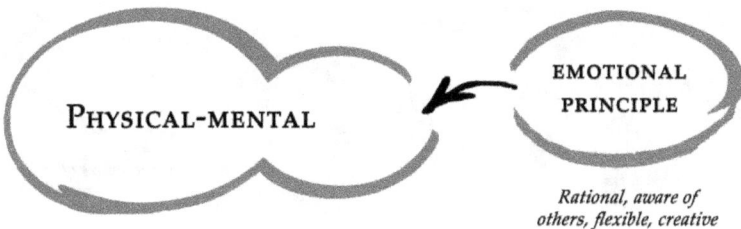

PHYSICAL-MENTAL → EMOTIONAL PRINCIPLE

Rational, aware of others, flexible, creative

For people with the Physical-mental process and for those with the Mental-physical process, it is the Emotional principle which is the third principle and has a need to be integrated into the person's development.

There is a natural ability to be detached and think logically in the two processes. It can make it so that they underestimate both their own and others' feelings and lose touch with them. It is important to be the one to make sure that rules are followed and no side-steps are taken from what has been decided. By activating the Emotional principle more, the person gains a greater understanding of one's own and others' feelings and can appreciate them. It is also easier to change plans and to become more flexible.

A person who has a Physical-mental process can go from being a rule-driven person with narrow and rigid values who finds it difficult to amend a decision, to becoming more flexible and speaking with his/her "personal voice". This will occur when the Emotional principle is integrated. This means that the person communicates to others his/her own values and opinions, and is able to tune in to views and feelings of others. When the principles interact, a greater awareness of the value of listening to others' opinions is gained. One can express one's personal concern more clearly, finding the right words, thereby contributing to a more open sharing of values.

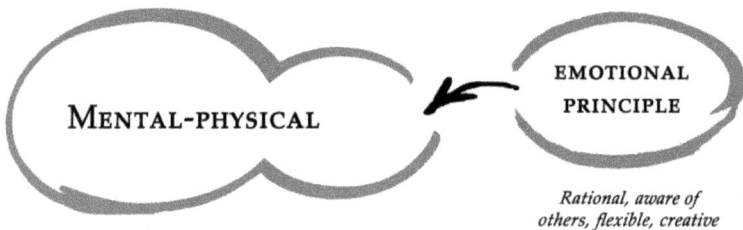

MENTAL-PHYSICAL

EMOTIONAL PRINCIPLE

Rational, aware of others, flexible, creative

The development path for people with the Mental-physical process can briefly be described like this. In the beginning of one's personal development path, a person can be enclosed in him/herself and show few emotional expressions. It is not so easy for others to interpret what he or she thinks or feels. One can easily get stuck in a narrow perspective without many personal contacts. When the Emotional part becomes more interactive with the other two principles, it becomes easier to make contact with others. It also becomes easier to understand and evaluate both one's own and other's feelings. One gets a greater subjective awareness of one's own person in relation to others.

As I have previously written, it seems that the third principle is a key to further growth and maturity. It is often the principle that recedes in situations of stress and uncertainty. When one is aware of his/her own process, training of the third principle results in a greater integration of the personality.

Even those who are not clear about their process can still practice all three principles. You can choose an exercise for the part you currently consider necessary to train.

The following exercises are compiled to train the Mental, Physical, and Emotional parts of our personalities, and you can choose what you think is best for you. The instructions are simple and clear. If you do the exercises frequently, you will soon realize what effect they have on your wellbeing. You can do them on your own or in groups. Always have paper, pen, and colors at hand. Exercises intended for a group are marked with an asterisk.

Exercises for your Mental principle

The Mental principle involves qualities such as detachment, structure, and selectivity. Detachment means that we need not allow ourselves to become involved in everything. We learn to set limits and keep perspective. Structure gives us the ability to focus on a task and not be fragmented and too multi-focused. When we can be selective, it helps us to choose from a wide selection of options, one or two activities instead of getting involved in too many things. It gives deeper knowledge and a higher quality in what we do.

EXERCISE 1

Sit on a chair where you can sit comfortably with your back straight. Close your eyes and take some deep breaths right down into the stomach area. Let the air pass through the nose and mouth, and feel how your body relaxes more and more, and how calmness spreads from the top of your head to the bottom of your feet.

Imagine a room with clean surfaces in a subdued color scheme. Few things are there, carefully selected and placed apart from each other. No one else is in the room. Stay in the room and let your mind rest. After a while, you can open your eyes and reflect on your experience.

You can choose to go into this room when you want to get greater clarity, focus, and distance to the world. You can use music with light, clear flute tones or violin music such as Paginini's Concerto 1 for the Violin; these are related to the Mental principle which has a high frequency (Seagal and Horne, 1997).

EXERCISE 2

Your Mental principle can also be practiced when you choose to paint an image in two colors based on a given pattern and try to reproduce it as accurately as possible. Work in silence in a methodical way. Other examples of exercises in painting are geometric figures and patterns. The purpose of this exercise is to accurately and precisely reproduce the pattern without going beyond the given framework.

EXERCISE 3

You can also use language to work on developing your Mental principle. Close your eyes and take some deep breaths, be calm and relaxed. Imagine that you are alone on top of a very high mountain. Give yourself time to explore the mountain top. How does it feel to be there? What words pop into your mind? Collect words that come to you and write them down, words that express your experience of being up there on the mountain top. Reflect for a moment on the words you have written, and see if you in some way can connect them to yourself and your Mental principle. The purpose of this exercise is to train the visual ability and be able to shift the focus to the part of yourself that may be relevant in a particular situation.

EXERCISE 4

Sit on a chair where you can have your back straight but still sit comfortably. Close your eyes and feel that you are relaxed and calm in your body. Check your breathing. How do you breathe? Will your breath come from deep inside your body or from the area around your heart? As you inhale, let your breathing become calm and still.

Now let your attention move to the area above your head. It may be just above your head, or higher. It is up to you. Let music with light tones of the flutist or violin play through you such as Paganini's music, which I earlier gave as an example supporting the development of the Mental part. Another example is Bach's Sonata No 3 in C major for violin and guitar.

How do you feel to have your attention directed above your head? Sit a while and be just in the space above you. When you open your eyes, write down your experience in a few short, clear sentences.

The aim of all these exercises is to give us the ability to greater stability, clarity, distance, and objectivity in what we think, feel, and do.

EXERCISES IN EVERYDAY LIFE.

Practice prioritization, be selective.

Ask yourself: "Of the eight things I want to do today, what are the four most important for me?" Then just do them and be satisfied with them.

When you feel emotionally overwhelmed, try to identify the feelings and then ask yourself: "What is behind these feelings?" To understand them, analyze them and try to lift them up onto your Mental plane.

If you find it difficult to speak with your personal voice, train yourself to say: "I do," "I do not understand," "I want," etc.

Practice setting boundaries, being clear in what you say, for example: "I do not have time to…" or "I do not want to participate in…" or "I cannot do what you ask me…"

Be with yourself in silence, perhaps outdoors. Allow yourself to work at your own pace, and do not let yourself get stressed by what is going on around you. Take a few deep breaths and let your breathing and pace interact in everything that you do. Another way to gain perspective is to meditate daily.

Exercises for your Physical principle

The Physical principle demonstrates the abilities and qualities related to implementation and overall making. To achieve a result, it is very important to carry out and complete a task. Patience to work closely and in detail and sensitivity to others are valuable properties.

EXERCISE 1*

Four people will together create an image. They have a large, rectangular piece of heavy paper (e.g., poster board). Each person holds a corner of the paper. Each person also has four small cups with different colors of paint (e.g. Redomix).

One person begins to spill one of the colors on the paper while the rest of the group in silence moves the paper up and down and sideways. One by one, each person spills one of their colors at a leisurely pace on the paper, all waiting their turn. There is a different color each time. They can go around the circle several times, depending on how they want their picture to look. When the image is complete, the group agrees on a name for their artwork. The whole exercise is completed with an exhibition from each group.

The purpose of the exercise is teamwork on the same terms, where the participants allow everyone to get space and where the communication is silent and as valuable as verbal communication.

EXERCISE 2

This exercise starts with you sitting on a chair and feeling the body's weight against the chair's back and seat. Close your eyes and take some deep breaths, and let the air pass through the nose and mouth. Note where your breathing is coming from. Is it from the stomach area, diaphragm, or chest? Feel in your body where your breathing is coming from. Breathe evenly and calmly.

Now imagine that you are a tree, a tree that has deep roots in the ground and which is steady. How does your tree look? Is it an old or young tree? Where is your tree, what are your surroundings like?

Choose words that belong to the ground and the earth when you experience your tree. Write down your words and paint a picture of your tree.

Then compare those words to the words you wrote in the exercise of the high mountain and the Mental principle.

The purpose of this exercise is to experience peace, continuity, and connectedness with our surroundings and ourselves, and to feel that we are part of the whole.

EXERCISE 3

Be quiet and still, become aware of your breathing and release the tension in your body. The music you are listening to now is something by Mozart. Be aware of the space both in front and behind you. Try to keep your attention in this space while the music plays.

The music we choose might be Mozart's Piano Concerto #21 or Bach's Concerto in D minor for two violins.

Do you feel that you want to move about? You can do it. What colors show up for your mind's eye? What words and images come to you?

When the music stops, and if you do this exercise together with others, sit together with two other participants while you talk and paint a picture of your experiences. If you do the exercise for yourself, you can make your own picture of your experience.

EXERCISES IN EVERYDAY LIFE

Stop five times every day and listen to your breathing. Practice breathing slowly with deep breaths.

When someone talks about a personal problem, train yourself to listen attentively to what the person is saying without offering a solution.

In a conversation, for example to practice patience, if someone is aggressive or very tedious, imagine that you can broaden your perspective and listen without being directly affected. The whole time breathe slowly and deeply, so that you will be calm and receptive to impressions.

When you are impatient to get on with a task, stop and ask yourself: "Have I completed what I am doing?" "Do I need to do something more to get it completely ready?" "Am I satisfied with what I have done?"

Exercises for your Emotional principle

When we train the Emotional principle, the most subjective and personal part of us, the feelings arise from one central location. We need to see and understand the qualities and abilities that are available in this principle. Abilities include communicating, building relationships with yourself and others, as well as flexibility, being able to break old patterns. Creative imagination allows us to create new things and see new paths.

EXERCISE 1*

The following exercise is conducted in silence, and it is about communication without words.

Each pair has together a piece of paper, some paint, and one brush.

The whole exercise is done without any exchange of words. One person starts spontaneously to paint something, and when he/she feels it appropriate, the brush is handed over to the other person who continues to paint.

During the exercise share the brush many times between each other in acceptance and love.

After completing the exercise, it is important to follow it up. What was easy with the exercise? What was difficult? How did it feel to turn over the brush to the other person?

The purpose of this exercise is to be aware of and able to meet others' needs and to share a task with them.

EXERCISE 2

Music can express the Emotional principle in different ways, depending on the situation and what you want to achieve.

In listening to music, our feelings and experiences are expressed, but also the part of our emotional lives that express the unconditional love that does not require something from another person, a more universal part of us.

Music suggested for this part is Chopin's flowing music: Nocturne Op. 9 #1 in B-flat minor, or Concerto #1 for Piano and Orchestra, or Op. 11 in E minor.

The language of the Emotional principle is expressed by the flow of our emotions. It can be descriptions of interactions with others, or more briefly, for example as in the Japanese Kokin Waka-shu Haiku poetry.

EXERCISE 3*

Participants are divided into groups of three to five people.

Each participant will get four blank 3 x 5" cards. On the front of each card write a feeling in one corner (e.g. anger, love, sadness, or the like).

The cards are dealt and laid on the table upside down.

The leader then asks participants to turn up one of their cards, while the others are left upside down.

In a few minutes (no longer) everyone should paint a picture of the word on the card based on the feeling that the word on the card triggers. After just a few minutes, the paintings are put aside, and the group turns to the next card and to do the same.

When everyone in the group has painted his/her emotional cards, you put the cards in front of them and each one shares their pictures with the group.

Emotional cards could also be used to create a poem or a sketch.

The purpose of the above exercise is to let everyone according to his/her own experience of the words, be able to express them. Through active listening, give participants space for each other without judging.

EXERCISE 4*

In the same way as in a previous exercise, you sit on your chair with your back straight. You are both relaxed and calm.

This time, you should have your attention directed towards the space available on each side of yourself out from your heart.

It is found that the music of Chopin supports the Emotional principle and helps us to experience the unconditional love. Examples of music you can listen to are Nocturne Op. 9 No 1 in B minor and Nocturne Op. 9 No 2 in B minor.

When the music stops playing write down your experience. If you are in a group, talk in pairs.

EXERCISES IN EVERYDAY LIFE

It can be several times during the day that you ask yourself: "How do I feel about this?" Listen carefully for the answers that come from within yourself.

Listen to a song and be aware of how your own emotions come into contact with the music. One idea could be to produce artwork, as painting your feelings, just let your painting flow to the tones of the music.

Practice informing others of your own thoughts even before you are finished what you are thinking. Ask questions to others. How do they perceive what you told them about?

Communicate by saying: "I feel this..." or "My sense of this is..."

Ask others how they perceive things and try to understand and put their feelings into words that you hear expressed.

You can keep a diary where you write down your feelings about a task or situation you are in.

You can listen for another person's feelings and ask questions about how the other person feels. Practice telling someone whom you are close to about your feelings.

Express your appreciation of others' efforts when you think it fit to do so.

When you give feedback, e.g. on the work of others, begin to praise what is right and good before talking about what could be done better.

There is always a reason to further emphasize the development of the Emotional principle within us. In the times we live in today, the development of the Mental and Physical parts reaches far beyond the Emotional part. Over several thousands of years, we have been able to refuel and create favorable conditions for survival. With intellectual clarity, we have made great technological advances to facilitate life and meet the physical and mental needs that exist. In physics and medicine, we have been able to conquer new lands, increase human longevity, and understand complex relationships between Earth and the Universe. We can travel to different places, using new technology and with the help of the computer, take us around the world in minutes.

The need to focus on our Emotional principle has been increasingly apparent in recent years. We are today talking about our "emotional intelligence", being social beings, having the ability to cooperate and show empathy. Qualities that we all have. Many times we act in a selfish and self-centered way rather than empathetic and loving for the benefit of each other. With greater awareness, we can train ourselves to highlight and develop the Emotional part of us.

We can also train ourselves to be relaxed and more open to trust our intuition. Intuition and intellect go hand-in-hand. Intellect supports our intuition when we have to solve problems or start a new job. Our intuition helps us find our way on unfamiliar roads and helps us to think new thoughts. In order to take advantage of our intuition, we must be aware of our own inner processes and allow the intuitive ability to find different ways to be expressed. We all have the ability to get in touch with and develop our intuition. When it is respected and valued, intuition can be a valuable tool.

Paul Brunton (1969), philosopher and thinker has written:

"Intuition is indeed taken from inside myself, whether it is about practical or spiritual things, whereas the intellect takes its conclusions from the facts that we acquire from outside. Intuition tells us what we should do. Reason says how we should proceed. Intuition indicates the direction and the target. Reason gives us a map of how to get there."

Transpersonal development

The personal development path has also another dimension which is more qualitative. Seagal and Horne (1997) argue that what they call transpersonal development is characterized by features that support the personality to be able to operate in a larger perspective beyond the self. Something that is important for more than one's own self. Just as in personal development, there are Mental, Emotional, and Physical aspects. The Mental part, which shows itself in our logical thinking, objectivity and perspective, is, in its transpersonal way, the ability to envision, not just for the person him/herself or for a small group, but in a broader perspective, e.g. humanity. We seek a more fair society. The transpersonal part of us humans can be a great source of inspiration to broaden our perspective and change how we relate to others through our own lives. People will immediately think about Mother Theresa, Nelson Mandela, and Martin Luther King, Jr., who all in their personal development became transpersonal to help to improve the world.

The Emotional principle, on a personal level, expresses the care and dedication of those who are close to us. In its transpersonal form, it gives a capacity for deep compassion, the kind of love and care that is not temporary but permanent and unconditional, which requires nothing back. When we act in an empathetic and compassionate way, without thought of personal gain, we do something for others and for humanity. Many of the volunteers who daily help vulnerable people are in different ways acting through the transpersonal part of their personality. Many times we have heard these people talk about the happiness and satisfaction they feel in doing good.

In the personal development of the Physical principle, we try to do what's best for the group and the individual. In the transpersonal act, our vision and objectives are anchored in a broader perspective that can serve others. Former President Barack Obama (2004) said in his book DREAMS FROM MY FATHER:

What is our community, and how might that community be reconciled with our freedom? How far do our obligations reach? How do we transform mere power into justice, mere sentiment into love? ... I find myself modestly encouraged, believing that so long as the questions are still being asked, what binds us together might somehow, ultimately, prevail. (p 438)

We all have the ability to develop and integrate the Mental, Emotional, and Physical parts at the transpersonal level. In the same way that the third part is the key to personal development, it is also the one that opens the way to the transpersonal. If the integration of the third principle is only done on a personal level, the difficulty will be to do it on the transpersonal. It is important that both the personal and the transpersonal development go hand-in-hand. Then we more consciously can use all of our power and capacities.

MY EXPERIENCE OVER MORE THAN 30 YEARS

The experience I want to share with you is naturally linked to my years as a school teacher and principal. It is mostly from the world of education that I gained some of my knowledge. If I had been working in another profession, I suspect that my experiences would have been different, and yet the descriptions of our various basic processes would still have been the same.

I personally believe that the basic processes are with us throughout life. The small child's specific needs are already apparent in the very young child. You can of course ask if they are an early character or if the personality already can be shown in the womb. When I have talked with parents about their children, I often have asked if they feel that their children are like each other or different in their way of being. Most of the time I get the answer that their children are different and have been right from their birth. They have different needs, e.g., their relationship with the parents and with others in their environment. The ways to play, communicate, and learn are also different in the early life of the children. Children in a family do not grow up under the same conditions and, of course, are influenced in different ways by their surroundings. This may involve the location of siblings, what expectations there are of them, and what roles they have in their home environment. The basic needs that children express are there, however, regardless of siblings, birth order, or in what environment they are growing up. Children are like flowers, and we adults their gardeners. It is our task to ensure that everyone gets the nutrients, water, and sunlight that they need.

Simon, so sensitive, so multi-focused, when the impressions were too many, too loud, it became too much, and he just ran around and around and screamed. Then it would be difficult to get in touch with him. There were simply too many impressions. As his parents knew him so well and knew how important it was to help shield him from the outside world, they could in different ways try to do that. This is something that small children need help with. Simon's parents chose not to have many activities during the weekend. If for example they were invited to somebody's home on both Saturday and Sunday, they chose only one of the days; the other day they stayed at home with the motivation: "There will be too many emotional impressions for Simon, he needs peace and quiet."

Instead of being in too many different activities where parents and children were running here and there trying to participate in as many activities as possible, the child who needs to be in a quiet and calm space should be given many opportunities during the day. The children themselves cannot express their needs. Children and parents then become more and more stressed and depressed. The children will react by becoming anxious, impossible to converse with, and in the end, they sit "on the ceiling." Then it can happen that one asks: "Can it possibly be ADHD or another disorder?" I think it is rather that it could be a protest from the child when he/she cannot cope with the environment.

When Gustav was little, he wanted not to approach other children. In the playground, it might happen that another child was glad to see him and came running to him. When the child wanted to show Gustav something, Gustav took several steps back, and looked at the other child without saying anything. In the sandbox, he sat by himself, and when a child came and took a toy from him, he did not protest; he looked down or away. If his parents had not known about Gustav's basic needs, they could have started to blame him for his behavior. Now, instead of worrying about it, they could give him conscious support for his way to develop. Since Gustav was not the only child who did not quickly establish contacts with others, his parents could explain to the other children about Gustav's needs and how he wanted to play in the playground that Gustav had chosen, and with whom he wanted to play. With their knowledge, they could meet his needs. Today he is a balanced and well-developed young man with no difficulties in communicating and interacting with others.

When we meet a child who is the same way as Gustav, who keeps a distance to his/her surroundings and does not communicate with others in the way we expect, we might judge the child as anti-social and impeded. Such an interpretation and misunderstanding can be devastating to the child.

One of my friends told me about her little grandson, who participated together with his mother in a singing group of young children when he was two years old. He sat in the ring with the other children and saw what happened. He did not take part in the songs. Both the teacher and the mother tried to get him to sing with the other children, but he was quiet and sat looking at the other children. Both his mother and the singing teacher thought that he did not participate because he did not understand the words of the songs. The mother even began to think that there might be something wrong with the boy's hearing. But such a surprise occurred when they came home after they had been at the song lesson for the fourth time, and the little boy suddenly began to sing all the songs, all the words and every one on the right note!

Perhaps it was simply that the boy had the Physical-emotional process and needed to collect all of his impressions, listen, and take in what was said and done. Not until he was finished with that could he act, namely singing. Think how many times we judge and misunderstand these children. When we believe that they do not have an answer to a direct question, or when we do not give them enough time to process the information they received, then we miss a lot of valuable knowledge.

A group of teachers in a school in southern Sweden decided to conduct their own internal investigation of the students who they thought might need special education. These were students that the teachers felt they did not quite reach in communication. They discovered that the students who were judged to need school support units and were receiving special education had different learning processes and communication needs than the teachers themselves. Could it be that when the teacher's process is completely different than the student's this can create learning difficulties which are interpreted as school or student difficulties? In an earlier chapter, I referred to C. Brooks in her study that demonstrated this (1987). Since I have long lived with the knowledge of the different processes, daily I have been able to avail myself of this knowledge in all sorts of contexts and situations. It has increasingly become a natural part of me when I meet people.

When I meet a person whom I feel I cannot reach in a conversation, I begin to ask myself: "Does this person have completely different communication needs than myself?" Without thinking about it more closely, I try to find the way to reach the person better. Sometimes I get irritated when a commentator or expert on the TV pronounces judgment so categorically about a famous person. It can be actors, politicians, or anyone else: "What if he could offer a little more of himself. He must show more commitment, more feelings, more passion. He takes a long time before he comes to a decision." Often, it is Emotionally centered people who speak out and criticize. How do they know that the person in question is not engaged and not showing that passion or commitment, even if he does otherwise than themselves?

A few months ago, I was in an ICA store near my home. As I walked around with my cart and selected my goods, I met a father with two young daughters in a twin stroller. The girls were so sweet, about two years old I think. I smiled at them and one girl replied immediately with a big smile back and direct eye contact. It was almost as if she stretched her arms towards me. The other little girl did not show any eye contact with me. She looked at me seriously and searchingly, and I could almost see that maybe she was thinking: "Who is that and what does she want?" My question to the father of the girls "Are the girls the same or different in their way of being?" He replied: "They are very different." He pointed to the first little girl and said that she was much more developed and socially mature than the other girl. I responded that I did not think it was because the first girl was more developed and more socially mature, but that the girls had a completely different way to experience their surroundings. I wanted to tell him more about our differences, but I understood that it was not appropriate to do that in the ICA store surrounded by shopping carts. After I left the store, I could not stop thinking about the two little girls. What signals are we adults sending to our children, often quite unconsciously? Do we hold that the norms and values of the wider community are what count? Maybe the second little girl who did not speak spontaneously and immediately to me will soon begin to see herself as not as valuable as her twin sister. This is something that can make its mark on her future life. Sure, over the years I have met people's skepticism and doubts regarding the description of our different basic processes. It could be someone who says: "It may not be as easy as just sorting people into different compartments and describing them based on that." When you speak out so, you have not understood or wanted to acquire sufficient knowledge. It is not about sorting or labeling people, but to have a tool that helps us to meet people's differences with greater openness, understanding, and joy. The interplay between the principles, their quantitative distribution and qualitative development gives everyone an unexpected opportunity to grow and develop.

PRACTICAL SUGGESTIONS

After completing the course, I sometimes got the question: "How should I start my practical work in the classroom?" I usually respond that the very first thing I start with is relaxation exercises. This is something that is a good gateway into the future work. Relaxation exercises help us create space to let feelings and thoughts come to mind. The effects will be a calmer climate, set a more focused work, and space to better listen to each other. Relaxation exercises benefit our personal development. We can, in a relaxed state, more easily come in contact with the Emotional, Physical, and Mental parts within us.

Therefore, I start my class every day with a relaxation exercise. Through that "we set the day" for further work during that day. "To set the day" was something I learned in a school in a nature reserve for the Native Indians in Canada. The Indian teacher told me that there was a need to create harmony and wholeness for the day's work, as well as to tie together the day before the students left the school.

In the National Association Home and School's magazine (October 2008) I read an article about the conscious exercise in relaxation. In a school in Stockholm, the students begin every day along with their teacher, making a ten-minute relaxation exercise. With a calm voice and tranquil music, the teacher leads the students through the exercise. When the journalist asked what the students thought about the relaxation exercise, one said: "During the relaxation, I try not to think at all." Another said: "When I feel stress, I think it is a good tool to get rid of the stress." The teacher said: "We let our thoughts be still." During the relaxation exercises this happens. She felt that it is a very good method. She felt that following the relaxation exercises the students had better focus on the task and completed their school day and school work in a more satisfying way.

At Orebro University, now the University of Orebro, Dr. Lars-Eric Unestahl, Ph.D., conducted a survey on how relaxation exercises affected the high school students' mental health. The survey showed significant differences between students who did the relaxation exercises daily and students who did not. The first group was shown to have improved mental health. The students' academic performance had also improved.

Learning environments based on the three principles

After many years, having been a teacher in special education and then a school leader, I turned back to the classroom as a teacher. One of the reasons was to apply my new knowledge about our basic Human Dynamics processes in practice. My 27 students in grade four met their new teacher in the fall semester's first day of classes with great curiosity. They got a teacher who wanted to be better prepared to meet her students' different needs and support them in their personal development.

Consciously, I tried more to remember to connect the three principles. To be more objective in the lesson's structure, facts, and visual experience (Mental). I also wanted to give opportunities for communication, creativity and new ideas (Emotional), and made sure that the background facts should be real and rooted together for cohesion and integrity (Physical).

After a number of weeks into the fall semester, my ideas of different learning environments began to take shape. I wanted to help my students meet their needs in their learning process. When you start working in learning environments do not try to change in too large of an area. Just take small steps. Otherwise, it may happen that which happened to me and my students. I was too eager to get started and gave too large and wide amount of data that the students themselves could choose from. They were totally free to choose without knowing about the learning environment in which they wanted to start. Most often they went to the environment that their best friend chose, even if it was not suited to be the best way for them to start. After a few weeks there was total confusion, and I had no opportunity to follow up on the students work. Some of them came crying to me and said: "We do not want to work this way; we want to do as we did before when we were in third grade." Then it was time for me to think and rethink!

I had put too much responsibility on the students too soon. I should have given them the opportunity to gradually train themselves in self-responsibility and understand the value and joy of learning new things in different ways. I realized that we changed our approach too abruptly. We needed to start with a well-structured work. It was mathematics. In the rest of the subjects we worked initially in a more traditional way. Gradually, when the students felt secure with the new approach, we could go on using different learning environments.

Learning environment based on the Mental principle

In this learning environment, it is essential to practice precision and accuracy, and to collect facts and structure. Access to computers, reference books, and materials will be provided. In the learning environment, you must give both clear and precise instructions to the different areas of work that are developed on a fact-oriented and objective manner. The instructions should be both written and oral.

Since starting on the basis of a visual work, you can make pictures and videos available related to the work area for the task. The colors in the room should be light and bright. There should be opportunities to work individually or in small groups.

The results of work made by students in this learning environment can be through presentations such as posters and/or by reading texts created from the given task.

Learning environment based on the Emotional principle

The Emotional principle learning environment is more colorful, with a diversity of different types of materials and colors. There may be a couch, a few comfy chairs around a table to sit in groups and talk. All this helps to provide for communications and dialogue to come up with creative new ideas, both in thought and in shape. Materials of all kinds must be available and inviting. The facts must be presented to students in a personal way. It may be an invitation to a theme of work, which is linked to students' own experiences and feelings about the work, where they have the opportunity to jointly present proposals for working methods, etc. Accordingly, in this learning environment the work can be presented individually or in groups. Students can agree on the form of the reports that can be done in many different ways.

Learning environment based on the Physical principle

In the Physical learning environment, different kinds of materials are accessible, preferably natural materials such as stones, pine cones, sand, shells, bird's nest, etc. Depending on the task or the theme, the idea is to work with different materials. Students learn through all of the senses to take in and to process the information.

There should be concrete materials especially in mathematics, but also in other subjects. Students should have the opportunity to connect the concrete and practical link to the theoretical. This is often done after they solve the task. When we work in mathematics, we work with units of measure, and let the students bake a cake where the recipe is to be followed and the cost of the cake calculated. This learning environment can also be a place to spend time. So as carefully as possible, describe the objects, the historical eras and make visible the practical results of the experiments. Be sure to give students the time and opportunity to present their work from a holistic perspective in their detailed and thorough manner.

Sometimes teachers resist changing their way of working. That is because we feel safe with the old methods. It has worked well, so why should we change? In a school, the teachers were initially opposed to dropping the old forms and doubted that their way of working needed to be changed. After a few years I revisited the school together with a group of school leaders and teachers from Singapore. I happily experienced the meeting with teachers and students.

We were met by cheerful and enthusiastic teachers who proudly showed us their learning environments. They spoke warmly about how good it was for the students to work and study here. Specifically, I think one of the male teachers (who was originally opposed to this change) showed how he rebuilt the entire library and created learning environments based on the three principles. During our visit there, the students were actively working on writing the school's newspaper. Documentation, interviews with teachers from

Singapore, and an appealing layout was what we were taking part in. Most of all, I remember the pride, joy and enthusiasm that existed among both teachers, school leaders, and students.

Working in groups

When we know people with different communication needs, we can more consciously make use of that knowledge in teamwork. To match the actual standard of a group, there are things you need to learn. Many groups of adults have difficulty interacting so that the process in the group is not optimum. There might be one or two who take command and control the whole group, and it becomes their ideas and viewpoints that emerge. There is no room for the other people to come into play. Thus, the others become more passive viewers and lose motivation for the task. The group acts as if has an IQ of 45, even if the individuals in the group have an average IQ of 100 (Senge, 1990).

Requirements for a group to work:

The members of a group must be aware of their own functioning and functioning of other members. They show respect and have a keen sensitivity for each other's processes. For everyone, feelings of security, acceptance, and responsibility should exist.

The following group exercise can be of value to apply when you want to train collaboration:

The group size should be no larger than 5-7 people. The group needs to get the task presented both orally and in writing.

Before the work starts, each one tells the others in the group about their strengths and what they think they could contribute in the future of the group. The group provides feedback and comes up with questions.

The members discuss design and implementation, and agree on who should lead the various parts of the work. The leadership can change among the members.

Before starting, select a timekeeper to keep time during the work. The rule is to make a stop after 30 minutes of meeting about the work/task. At that time, each one writes down their answers to the following questions:

How do I work in the group?

Do I contribute with my abilities in the work? If not, why not?

What can I do to support the work of the group?

After a brief self-reflection on the responses, each member shares his/her thoughts with the rest of the group. After that the work will continue and you can again make an additional stop for reflection. The entire group work may last 60-90 minutes, depending on what the work assignment is.

In a group, it is common for all to focus on the result of what the work should be. It is good, but equally important to focus on the process and to develop the group and know what happens there. Can all members be seen? Do all members get their thoughts and opinions heard? Were the group members a support for each individual member of the group? Did the process that evolved have a significant impact on the outcome?

The purpose of this exercise is that everyone in the group become more aware of how important the group process is, and to create a desire to take advantage of each one's abilities and to learn from each other. This makes the work more interesting, more qualitative, where different aspects and ideas can come into the group work.

REFLECTION

One can ask the question: "Has the person's process been a creation of different cultures or do the cultures create each person's basic different process. I look forward to the day when we know more, when researchers in different disciplines can show if these processes are genetic or influenced very early by the culture we live in. Researchers today lean more and more towards the finding that we are born with basic personalities. In *Science Illustrated* (NR18/2008), we learned about the Big Five: five personality qualities, based on extroversion, relaxation, ingenuity, empathy, and openness. The researchers of Big Five found that all people have these qualities, but they are expressed with different weights and in different ways in various people.

The presence of the five personality dimensions is also supported by recent neurological research. In *Health and Science* (No. 2/2010) Paul Lichtenstein, a professor of genetic epidemiology at the Karolinska Institute, states that in the beginning of his research, he was only focused on the environment and cultures which have a strong effect on humans. When he got his results, which demonstrated that some of the properties were hereditary, he changed his focus to also include the hereditary factor. At that point, many people were skeptical. Yet today he says that it is quite the contrary. Now most believe, with evidence, that there are definite inheritable properties. For me, it always has been the children in the center, and sometimes I have felt overwhelmed by being the one piloting them through childhood and adolescence. What a profound responsibility it is to be a teacher. In the late 1980s when I began to apply my knowledge of our various basic processes, I saw how my many students came to know their way of being, and then I knew that I had found a key that opened new doors.

Our basic processes are universal. It is all about being human. Wherever you are and whatever you do, the knowledge is valuable to have. Even if you cannot interpret people's different basic processes, you can come to know your own way of being and how to relate to others in a more open and tolerant way. As an educator, you can more consciously provide the conditions to allow students to choose different ways and be supportive of their choice. If you notice that someone does not understand an instruction or cannot answer a question, try to ask the question in a new way or explain the task differently. You can find your way and experiment with questions. The communication and interaction mean that we can meet each other with respect and create a learning environment, a prerequisite for learning.

The starting point for this book was when Simon asked me to write about our processes so that his friends would understand themselves and others better. The teens are creating an identity to understand themselves and get to know who they are. If we could have words for the qualities and abilities that each one has and learn to appreciate them early on in our lives, imagine what strength, self-awareness, and self-esteem it would provide. By taking part in the various process descriptions and starting to think about oneself, one can better understand why we react as we do in different situations. Balanced interplay of the three principles teaches us to deal with our thoughts, feelings, and actions in an appropriate manner.

If in the end we sum up with one word what the knowledge about our processes is about, it would be *awareness*. To understand and know oneself is a mission for all people. Our approach to life is dependent on the perception we have about ourselves. It is therefore particularly important that we begin to understand and accept each other. We must try to look at ourselves and others with love, knowing that we are all OK, and that we all have the ability and responsibility to grow. When we can see the uniqueness of each human being, but also see what unites us, diversity is truly an asset.

REFERENCES

Bergström, B. (2001) *Every Child has Specific Needs*. Runa Förlag, Stockholm.

Bergström, B. & Saarukka, S. (2004) *The Pedagogic Tango*. Runa Förlag, Stockholm.

Brooks, C. (1987) *The Circle of Learning, Learning Styles in Native Adult Education Programs*. Ministry of Skills Department, London Ontario, Canada.

Brunton P. (1969) *The Secret Path*. Originally published in 1935, later part of a 16-volume set published by Swedish-American publisher Robert Larson in 1984.

Dunn, R. & Dunn, K. (1992) *Bringing out the Giftedness in Your Child*. John Wiley & Sons, New York.

Gardner, H. (1991) *The Unschooled Mind*. Basic Books, New York.

Gardner, H. (1993) *Frames of Mind*. Basic Books, New York.

Grodal R. N. (1990) *Forandring Fryder? Om mennesker og organisasjoner i omstilling*. J.W. Cappelens Forlag, Lillehammer, Norway.

Hoffman, B. (1972) *Albert Einstein Creator & Rebel*. The Viking Press Inc., NY, USA.

Obama B. (2004) *Dreams from my Father*. Crown Publishers, New York, NY, USA.

Seagal, S. & Horne, D. (1997) *Human Dynamics, A New Framework for Understanding People and Realizing the Potential in Our Organizations.* Pegasus Communications Inc. Cambridge, MA, USA.

Seagal, S., Horne, D., and Bergström B. (1999) Educational materials: *"Learning in different ways".* Human Dynamics International, Los Angeles. USA.

Seagal, S. & Horne, D.(2004) *The Book of Human Dynamics.* Runa Förlag, Stockholm.

Senge, P. M. (1990) *The Fifth Discipline,* Doubleday, New York.

Svedberg, L. (2003) *Group Psychology,* Student literature.

Active Magazine, *Home and School,* October 2008, Tyresö.

Health and Science Magazine, Popular science magazine from Läkartidningen, no. 2, May, 2010, Stockholm.

Illustrated Science Journal, no.18, 2008.

Vos, J. & Dryden, G. *The Learning Revolution.* Torrance, California, & Auckland, New Zealand: The Learning Web.

Vygotskij Lev S. (1999) Vygodskij and the School. Student literature.

Website, Wikipedia, Haiku poetry, Kokin Wakashú.

ABOUT THE AUTHOR

Berit Bergström is a former teacher, special education teacher, and has been working as a school leader for many years. Since the mid-1990s, she has worked on continuing education and skills development in preschools, schools, organizations, and business.

www.ingramcontent.com/pod-product-compliance
Lightning Source LLC
Chambersburg PA
CBHW051431090426
42737CB00014B/2917